Amul's INDIA 3.0

CONCEPT AND CREATION BY daCUNHA COMMUNICATIONS
BASED ON 50 YEARS OF AMUL ADVERTISING
BY daCUNHA COMMUNICATIONS

Harper
Collins

The profits from the sale of this book will be used to honour deserving Class X and XII students in India under the Amul Vidyashree and Amul Vidyabhushan Awards.

First published in India in 2012 by Collins Business
An imprint of HarperCollins *Publishers* India
This revised and updated edition published in 2016
by HarperCollins *Publishers* India

P-ISBN: 9789352641406
E-ISBN: 9789352641413

2 4 6 8 1 0 9 7 5 3 1

Created by: daCunha Communications

Editor: Meher Marfatia
Designer: Kermin Colaço

HarperCollins *Publishers*
A-75, Sector 57, Noida, Uttar Pradesh 2011301, India
1 London Bridge Street, London SE1 9GF, United Kingdom
Hazelton Lanes, 55 Avenue Road, Suite 2900, Toronto, Ontario M5R 3L2
and 1995 Markham Road, Scarborough, Ontario MIB 5M8, Canada
25 Ryde Road, Pymble, Sydney, NSW 2073, Australia
195 Broadway, New York, NY 10007, USA

Printed and bound at
Replika Press Pvt Ltd.

Acknowledgements

Who would have thought a campaign created in 1966 could withstand the test of time – and Twitter – to become the longest-running billboard campaign of all time. This third edition of *Amul's India* attempts to capture that journey.

For this book I am grateful to many people.
To my father Sylvester daCunha who created the 'Utterly Butterly Delicious' slogan. And, with art director Eustace Fernandes, conceived the little girl in a polka-dotted dress who slips seamlessly between being a commentator, cheerleader and caustic observer.
To the visionary Dr V. Kurien, who saw the potential in this idea and gave my father his blessings and freedom to create.

To my team at daCunha Communications. Devjit Kohli for his rock steadiness. Gopi Bagai for the co-ordination. And Dhiral Mehta for the conversion of low to high resolution of all the topicals featured in the book. To Praveen Bhandary of Origem for deftly dtp-ing the content to readable lucidity.

To my two brothers-in-arms, Manish Jhaveri and Jayant Rane – Manish for his skill and consistency as a writer over twenty-three years. And Jayant, cartoonist extraordinaire for thirty years.

To Meher Marfatia – writer and publisher (49/50 Books) in her own right – for whom editing and curating this complex book was no easy task. As well as to cajole twenty-five busy wordsmiths to deliver to deadline.
To Kermin Colaço (Carmma Ideas) – for the outstanding design of the book. From font to fun-filled graphics, her visual mastery has lit up every page.
Kermin and Meher in tandem prove the axiom – one plus one equals three.
Thank you both.

And finally to my wonderful clients at Amul, Messrs R.S. Sodhi, Kishore Jhala and Jayen Mehta, who encourage and trust us on a daily basis to express ourselves freely. It takes very special clients to foster this. Thank you, gentlemen. Bon voyage, dear reader.

Rahul daCunha

Contents

Foreword

R.S. SODHI
Managing Director
Gujarat Co-operative Milk Marketing Federation Ltd
Anand, Gujarat.

It gives me great pleasure to introduce the third edition of this book as the record-breaking print runs of the first and second editions have sold out. The accolades for the previous editions have been overwhelming and the clamour for 'more' of the iconic Amul girl's antics has continued unabated.

The Amul girl and the humorous hoardings she adorns have been an important ingredient in building the Amul brand. This book commemorates fifty years of her existence – and yet she seems as young, fresh and relevant as she was when it all began.

Amul emerged as an offshoot of the Indian freedom movement, to give poor farmers the best returns for their milk by eliminating middlemen. Since then it has grown into a national brand that is respected and trusted in every corner of the country. The purest milk products and interesting new formats and formulations as well as the concept 'Taste of India', the Amul moppet, and the consistent advertising strategy have all contributed to the Amul success story.

A daily and essential food product has to provide the consumer with the confidence that it is not only tasty and nutritious, but that it is produced to the highest hygienic standards, and provided at a fair and acceptable price. This is the assurance that the Amul brand promises, and for seventy years now, we have striven continuously to honour this commitment. We have renewed this by meeting, and often surpassing, the customer's expectations of quality, value for money, choice, availability and service.

This has been possible with the co-operation and combined efforts of a producer-owned and -controlled integrated system of production, procurement, processing and marketing.

This book portrays how an endearing moppet and her tongue-in-cheek humour helped a milk producers' co-operative create a 'white revolution'. It traces how Amul evolved as a brand by commenting on the popular political and social culture of India over the past five decades. Its topical, humorous and memorable hoardings continue to delight generations of Indians. DaCunha Communications has been the longest-ever partner of the Gujarat Co-operative Milk Marketing Federation (GCMMF) and is the creator of its Amul hoardings.

DY Works has partnered Amul in the last decade through brand creation and rejuvenation, and conceived, designed and created the first two books. This third book has been conceived, designed and created by daCunha Communications. It goes beyond being an ordinary anthology to being a chronicle of India through the eyes of the Amul girl. The multiple contributions by prominent writers and thinkers add to its richness.

Amul will continue to participate in the development of the country by using all the profits from the sale of this book to honour deserving Class X and XII students in India under the Amul Vidyashree and Amul Vidyabhushan Award schemes, just as it had done with the sales of the first two editions.

ONE DROP

TO OPERATION FLOOD

MILK

The Amul story

Anand, once a dusty, serene farming village, is today a symbol of modern nationalism. What started in 1946 in a village in Gujarat as a small co-operative effort to bring economic freedom to farmers by releasing them from the clutches of self-serving middlemen, has developed into a movement that involves millions of farmers all over the country, and into an incredible Rs 33,000 crore (US$ 5 billion) co-operative enterprise!

Anand is today the headquarters of the Gujarat Co-operative Milk Marketing Federation Ltd (GCMMF) and brand Amul.

A small fledgling co-operative has developed into a phenomenal movement. Each day, milk is collected at centres within easy reach of the farmer, thus easing the burden on him or her and ensuring that the milk is fresh. It is tested for quality and fat content on computerized equipment, making the process both fair and transparent. Cash payments are made based on the fat content of the milk, thus helping the farmer with his day-to-day requirements. A significant feature is that milk is purchased largely from women, thus economically and socially empowering them, and giving them a measure of influence in decisions regarding their welfare and development.

After independence, dedicated leaders heralded a new democratic consciousness, and encouraged measures to accelerate the pace of progress. The foundation stone for the major dairy in Kaira was laid by Dr Rajendra Prasad, the first president of India, and it was inaugurated in 1955 by Pandit Jawaharlal Nehru.

When invited to commission the cattlefeed plant at Anand in 1964, Prime Minister Lal Bahadur Shastri wished to spend one night at a farm, unaccompanied by anyone. Hesitantly, Dr Verghese Kurien, founder of GCMMF, took on this task. Shri Shastri and Dr Kurien sneaked out to a village where farmer Ramabhai and his family welcomed their guest, unaware that he was the prime minister! Next morning, a relieved Dr Kurien met Shri Shastri, who had spent the night talking to farmers about their lives and problems, and their experiences with the co-operative movement. So impressed was he that he requested Dr Kurien to replicate this in the rest of the country. Thus was born the National Dairy Development Board, headquartered at Anand. For the first time, a national institution was located in an obscure village rather than in India's capital city.

Dedicated freedom fighters with integrity and a vision for the future, such as Tribhuvandas Patel, Sardar Vallabhbhai Patel and Morarji Desai, brought with them a realization that the true development of India must begin at the grassroots. They mobilized the collective strength of the farming community under the guidance of enthusiastic and devoted professionals like Dr Kurien and H.M. Dalaya, and well-wishers like Maniben (daughter of Vallabhbhai Patel), and forged relationships beyond the merely professional. The primitive and basic rural working and living conditions encouraged a feeling of co-operation and caring amongst the largely city-bred professionals working together towards a common goal. Coming together in warm-hearted and selfless friendship were the Kuriens, the Variavas and Maniben, among others.

AMUL MODEL OF **MILK CO-OPERATIVES**

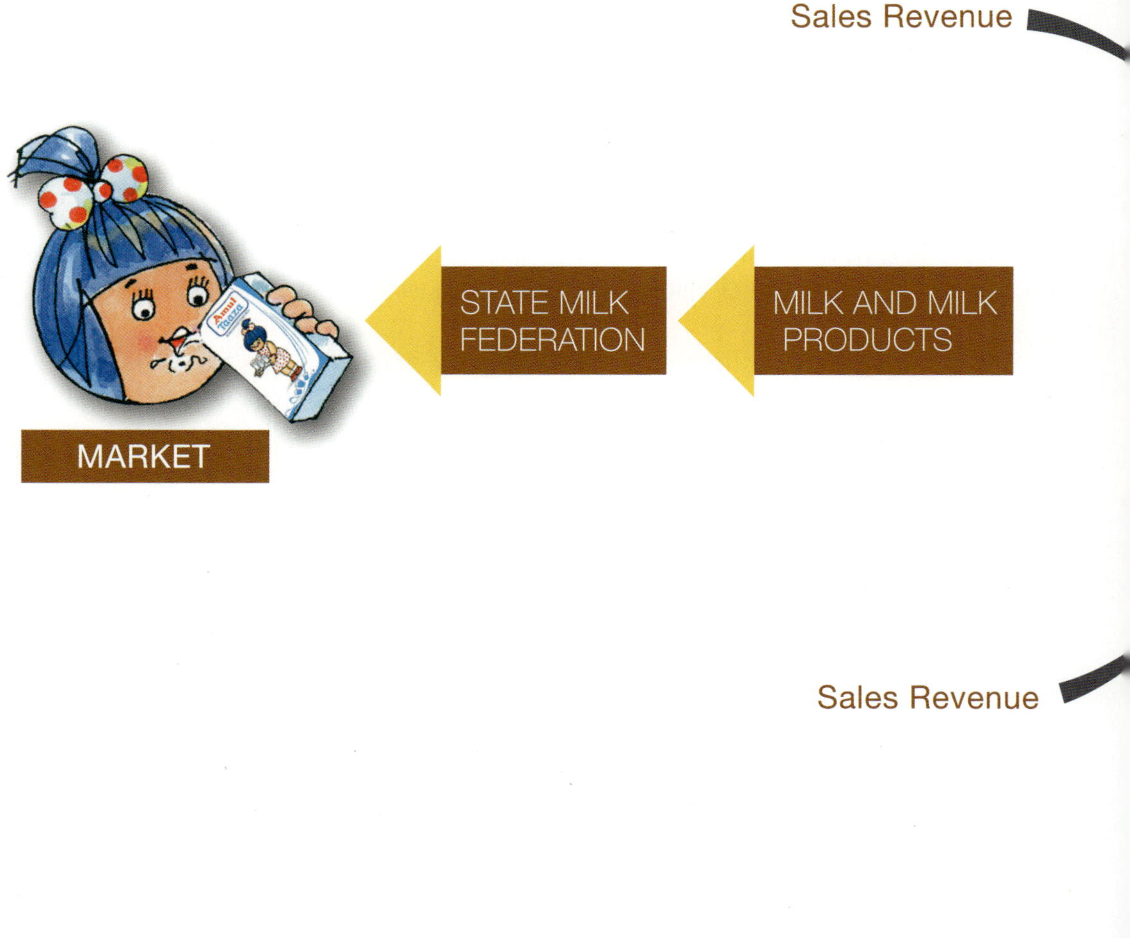

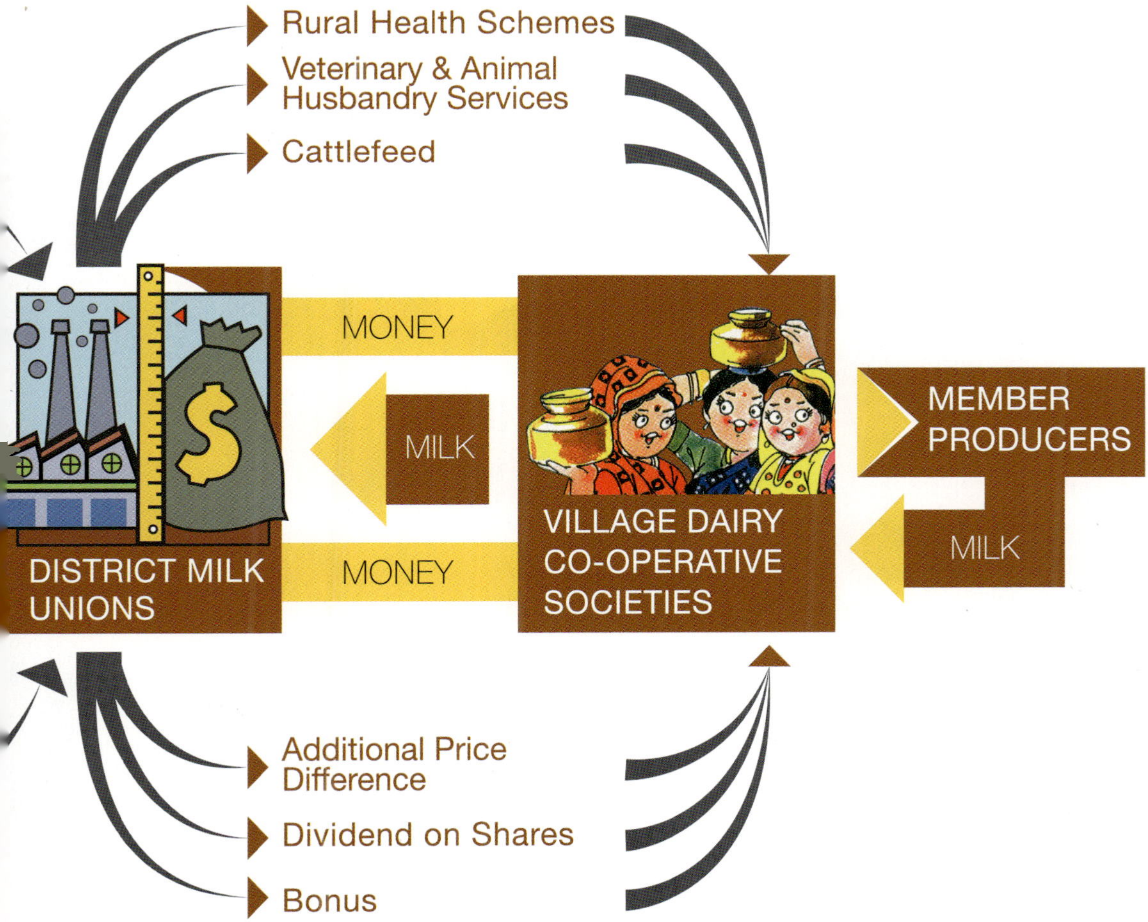
Rural Health Schemes
Veterinary & Animal Husbandry Services
Cattlefeed
MONEY
MILK
MONEY
DISTRICT MILK UNIONS
VILLAGE DAIRY CO-OPERATIVE SOCIETIES
MEMBER PRODUCERS
MILK
Additional Price Difference
Dividend on Shares
Bonus

DR VERGHESE **KURIEN**

(1921 - 2012)

Dr Verghese Kurien was the founder of the Gujarat Co-operative Milk Marketing Federation and the brain behind the development and success of the brand Amul. He was known as the father of the White Revolution in India and the architect of Operation Flood, which is the largest dairy development programme in the world.

Dr. Verghese Kurien

From the milkman of India

In a brief interview two years before he passed away, Dr V. Kurien shared some of his thoughts on the popular and much-loved Amul campaign.

Dr Kurien, this was a campaign that you initiated and gave your blessings to forty-six years ago and have supported through the years. What are your thoughts?
DVK: While the brand 'Amul' was registered in 1957, the advertising campaign started only in 1966-67. The Gujarat Co-operative Milk Marketing Federation, which markets the 'Amul' brand, came into being only about eight years later. Long before that, I realized that if we wanted to hold our own in the market, the professional services of an advertising agency were vital. My brother-in-law, K.M. Philip, very astutely advised us to leave the business of advertising to the experts, and that's what we did. Looking back, I realize how wise a decision it was to give complete freedom to the ad agency to do their job in a professional way. I never interfered with their work and the result is before you. They have done an exemplary job.

What do you feel the Amul girl has done for the brand?
DVK: The Amul girl has given the brand just the image we had in mind – that of a precious, 'priceless' product that the consumer could trust completely.

Do you have any personal favourites among the hoardings?
DVK: It is difficult to choose one hoarding over the others; each one of them is on contemporary subjects close to the heart of the general public, and quite unique. They are also very witty, thought-provoking and humorous.

Our tribute to the Father of the White Revolution.

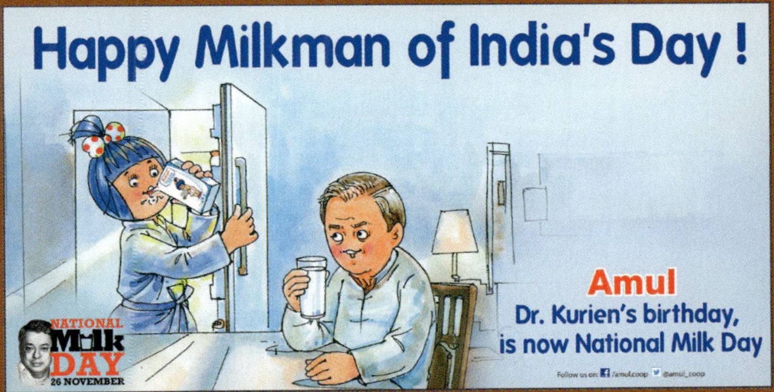

Dr Kurien's birthday, 26 November, was declared National Milk Day.

Celebrating the legacy of the Milkman of India's ninety-fourth birth anniversary.

SYLVESTER **daCUNHA**

Sylvester daCunha is the chairman of daCunha Communications Pvt Ltd. In 1966, he co-created the Amul butter hoarding campaign, heralding the birth of the longest-running outdoor campaign of all time.

The utterly butterly stry

It was 1966. The advertising for a product called Amul butter was assigned to an agency of which I was the manager. The butter had been on the market for about ten years. It was positioned as, 'processed from the purest milk under the most hygienic conditions by a dairy co-operative in Gujarat'.

This was like a lantern lecture to an indifferent audience. Nonetheless, it had left some positive impressions about the brand. But clearly, some pep needed to be injected into the communication.

For a start, we needed a tag line to replace 'Purely the Best.' A new slogan dropped out of the sky when I told my wife Nisha about our new ad assignment. She spontaneously remarked, 'Why don't you say "Utterly Amul."' To which I added, 'Hey, what about, "Utterly Butterly Amul!"' And so was coined a slogan that became one of the more memorable battle cries in advertising.

But the word 'butterly' initially met with some scepticism. 'It's ungrammatical,' objected a few. But Dr V. Kurien, the head of Amul,

A jockey holding a slice of buttered toast appeared during the horse-racing season.

said, 'I think it's utterly mad; but if you think it'll work, go ahead.' So there we had a very promising selling line. What we now needed was a spokesman to voice it. But who? Instinctively, I sensed it should be a child, someone impish and loveable. I explained this to my then art director, Eustace Fernandes, a brilliant visualizer and cartoonist. After a few tries he came up with this charming little poppet in a polka-dotted frock and a matching ribbon in her pony tail. She was licking her lips as though to say, 'Utterly butterly delicious.' Yes, she had all the qualities I was groping for – naughty, cuddly, innocent, smart. I knew we had a winner.

The lassie and her line first appeared on a few lamp-post boards in Mumbai. The public response was immediate: 'How cute!' So we decided to build an outdoor campaign around her. Hoardings as a medium are impactful if the locations are well chosen and the message compelling. Our very first display presented the missy praying by her bedside: 'Give us this day our daily bread – with Amul butter.' The feedback was very positive.

During the horse-racing season came 'Thoroughbread,' with a small jockey holding a slice of buttered toast. During the monsoons: 'Pitter-patter, pick-a, pack-a Amul butter.'

Calcutta in the 1960s was in the grip of hartals, with processions yelling 'Cholbe na!' ('Will not do!'). We turned that around to: 'Toast without Amul – Cholbe na! Cholbe na!' It drew a smile from many die-hard leftists.

The Hare Krishna movement was the target of an Amul jibe. 'Hare Rama, Hare Krishna – Hare Hare!' became: 'Hurry Amul, Hurry Butter – Hurry! Hurry!'

The Hare Krishna movement was the target of an Amul jibe.

Slowly, we found we were exploiting situations which were current. But topical ads pose a challenge. They need to appear immediately after the issue breaks out; else they lose their immediacy. The news of 100 runs by a cricketing hero or the crowning of an Indian Miss World needed an immediate Amul response. But the logistics of ad release ordinarily took time – first identifying the topic, then creating the rough layout, presenting it to the client, incorporating client's suggestions, often re-presenting for client's final approval; only then making multiple artworks for distribution to hoarding contractors, who erected scaffolds for painters to climb and do the needful. It could all take a week or more – much too long.

Dr Kurien, an inspiring client, immediately saw the need to cut corners. He told the agency that they were free to operate without obtaining his okay. That was a rare gesture indeed, but it reflected his unique way of going about things – the same uniqueness that made him the father of the milk revolution.

Dr Kurien did, however, caution us not to step on people's toes – 'If you get into trouble because of your ads, be prepared to face the music by yourself.' But when we did sometimes ruffle feathers, he stood by us.

The controversial decision by London airport authorities on virginity tests on Indian women was the subject of a billboard.

For instance, during a prolonged airline strike, a little uniformed air hostess said: 'Indian Airlines serves Amul butter – when it flies.' A furious airline demanded the immediate removal of the ad or threatened to stop serving Amul butter. Dr Kurien barked, 'The ad stays. No one's going to tell me how to run my advertising.' There were a few other instances when our ads were controversial. London airport authorities had taken a decision to conduct virginity tests on Indian ladies to verify their claims of having husbands already resident in the UK. We had spoofed: 'Indian virgin needs no urgin'!' Offended protests were immediately heard from women's rights groups. We apologetically blanked the message to avoid offence to our sisters.

There have so far been over 4,000 utterly butterly hoardings. This is probably the only campaign in the world with theme and style unchanged in fifty years.

You might say that they are like a history of modern India acted out by a little heroine, healthy and confident about the future.

The topical elicited furious protests from women's rights groups – so we extended a huge apology, Amul style!

SHYAM **BENEGAL**

Well-known film-maker Shyam Benegal popularized a new genre of Indian cinema and has won several national awards. He has been honoured with the Padma Shri, the Padma Bhushan and the Dadasaheb Phalke Award for lifetime contribution to Indian cinema.

The

smart-assed little girl with

the **fringe**...

My association with ASP (Advertising and Sales Promotion Company) goes back to January 1964 when I joined the agency. Sylvester daCunha (who headed the agency) and Usha Katrak (who handled the Amul account) jointly created the Amul butter campaign. There were some excellent creative people in ASP at the time. Sylvester was always buzzing with creative ideas, which were ably visualized by Marie Pinto and Eustace Fernandes. It was Eustace who visualized the smart-assed little girl with the fringe on top. The slogan 'Utterly butterly delicious' was Sylvester's creation.

Amul, which has now become synonymous with all milk products in India, actually began with Amul butter, and the Amul girl was created as a rival to the village belle of Polson's butter. Today, she has become a mascot for practically all Amul products despite Amul's attempts to see her as a mnemonic for their butter.

There was no television in the 1960s, and the only media available for advertising were press, outdoor, cinema and radio. For the radio,

Today, the Amul girl has become a mascot for practically all Amul products despite Amul's attempts to see her as a mnemonic for their butter.

The Amul moppet today, behind a backdrop of a hand-done strip dating from the early 1970s.

a jingle was composed by Nathan, who was extremely popular those days. The jingle he composed was used for radio as well as for film commercials for a long time. A few years later, my daughter Pia, who had just started her kindergarten, gave her voice for the line 'Utterly butterly delicious,' which eventually became the signature of all radio and film advertising.

When I gave up advertising to become an independent film-maker, I was often called upon to make film commercials for Amul.

Amul baby food had just come into the market and much like outdoor hoardings that were primarily used for butter, baby food was advertised using film commercials. This was a time when people believed only cow's milk was fit for baby food. Amul baby food was different. It was made from buffalo milk. The man who changed the equation was Dr V. Kurien. An extraordinary figure in the milk co-operative movement, he led the way to make India the largest milk-producing nation in the world, a feat achieved in a span of no more than twenty-five years.

The year 1965 was a very difficult one for India. We had barely recovered from the India-China War of 1962, when we were locked in armed conflict with Pakistan. Our resources were being drained and famine loomed large on the horizon. For Prime Minister Lal Bahadur Shastri, raising agricultural production in India became the top priority. He coined the now-famous slogan, 'Jai Jawan, Jai Kisan,' at the time. One hugely successful programme then was the milk co-operative movement in Gujarat, under the leadership of Dr Kurien.

Shastri wanted to replicate Amul's success in all other parts of India. This signalled the birth of the National Dairy Development Board (NDDB), and on Dr Kurien's insistence, it had its head office in Anand, which was home to Amul.

The birth of NDDB triggered the milk revolution in the country. An ambitious programme called Operation Flood was launched by Dr Kurien to help accelerate milk production in the country by creating milk co-operatives in all the milk sheds in the country.

I produced two documentary films on the two phases of Operation Flood. During the course of research and shooting of these documentaries, I realized there were many human interest stories that could be turned into a feature film. Mapping the stories of the farmers would be much more persuasive and entertaining to general audiences.

Dr Kurien did not need too much convincing. In fact, he came up with a novel way of raising money, by getting the farmers themselves to produce the film *Manthan* (The Churning). The film turned out to be a huge success with cinema audiences and also with farming and rural communities. Nothing could have been more satisfying for a film-maker like myself than to see a film succeed where it mattered most.

It has been my privilege to have known and worked with Dr Kurien.

JUG **SURAIYA**

Jug Suraiya is a writer, columnist, cartoonist and the author of several books.

Half a
century
of spreading
good
cheer

Many years ago, when she was a little kid, my niece Sheila was a cheeky brat, particularly so at the breakfast table. When her mother, my older sister Vasu, would serve the buttered toast on a platter, Sheila would grab a couple of slices, lick the butter off them and return the now-unbuttered toast to the serving dish.

'Why don't you also eat the toast?' I'd ask.

'Because butter tastes better than the toast,' she'd reply, helping herself to another slice.

Sheila's was an emphatic – if not necessarily elegant – endorsement of the peculiar seductiveness of butter.

Proust – of whom neither Sheila nor I had heard at the time – might also have been a butterholic. Who's to say it wasn't the butter in the madeleine which he ate that opened the floodgates of memory and led to his writing his monumental seven-part novel, *Remembrance of Things Past*, after which Literature with a capital L has never quite been the same again.

There is something about butter – soft and mellow-gold as winter sunshine – that evokes nostalgia. I used to live in what was then called Calcutta, and during school holidays, I'd go to visit my sister Vasu in what was then Bombay.

One of the many highlights of my Bombay holidays was the buttered toast at breakfast, Sheila's table manners notwithstanding. Bombay butter tasted different from Calcutta butter.

In Calcutta, we bought our butter from a genial young Bengali who ran a small shop in Bhowanipur's Jadu Babu's Bazar. He'd open his ice-box – no refrigerator in Jadu Babu's in those days – and take out a large slab of home-made butter. Using a wooden spatula, he'd carve off the quantity we wanted, which was wrapped in a banana leaf for us to take home.

In Bombay, our butter was bought from a Parsi gentleman who owned a store near the Eros cinema. Instead of in an ice-box, Bombay butter was kept in a refrigerator and came pre-packed in stiff grease-proof paper.

I could never quite make up my mind which of the two butters – the Calcutta or the Bombay – I liked more.

Such dilemmas were soon to be resolved. At about the time that political India was asking itself the question, 'After Nehru, who?' gastronomic India was asking, 'After Anchor, what?'

Anchor, of course, was the Australian-origin butter imported into India via Britain. The British having upped anchor and quit India to go home, how long before Anchor quit Indian shelves to be

This billboard was in protest against the frequent hartals in the Calcutta of the 1960s.

replaced by God-alone-knows-what substitute to spread on bread to make the wafer-thin cucumber sandwiches that were *de rigueur* at tea time everywhere from Altamount Road to Alipore, from Ballygunge to Bandra?

Fortunately, deliverance was shortly at hand, thanks to a swadeshi avatar of Anchor, which also began with an A and which was just as good, if not better, than the Aussie import. Not only did the newcomer taste good, it came with a bonus in the form of catchy, topical humour encapsulated in cartoons featuring a couple of cute kids.

Humour? As a marketing aid for butter? What if the product became the butt – or, in this case, the butter – of its own jokes? A bit risky, no?

And the short answer to that – which has stood the test of fifty years – is exactly that: No. Far from being a risky undertaking, the product's punny and pithy sales campaign has earned pride of place in the

ANCHOR'S AWAY!

UTTERLY, BUTTERLY SWADESHI-LICIOUS

advertising industry's hall of fame. One of the reasons for its success might be that there is an innate compatibility between butter and humour: both are wholesome and both help to spread good cheer.

While butter is good for the body physical, tasteful and inoffensive humour is good for the body politic. This holds true, more than ever before, perhaps, at a time when there seems be an epidemic of a new form of allergy called sensitivitis.

All sorts of people are contracting acute bouts of sensitivitis, a condition in which one's ideological/political/religious/ethnic/any, all or none of the above sensitivities, are hurt by what someone else says or does.

Sensitivitis is a painful ailment, and the best known antidote for it is humour. Good, clean, inoffensive humour, with malice towards none, which helps us to laugh with each other, and not at each other. In this case, humour that is as zestful and tasteful – in all senses of that term – as the product it so appropriately represents.

And what might that product be? It could be a brand of butter. Equally, it could be the laugh-and-let-laugh spirit of democracy itself.

As a combination, what could be more utterly, butterly delightful?

Partho Sengupta

HUMOUR

IN A HEADLINE

BACHI **KARKARIA**

Bachi Karkaria is an author, columnist, media trainer and Director, Times Litfest.
Alec Smart is the sign-off line of her column, Erratica, in *The Times of India*.

When Alec met Amuli

It was a love-hate relationship. In the real world, it could be a criminal perversion and the old boy would be clapped into jail. Alec Smart, age indeterminate but old enough to be cynical. Lanky. Dressed in jeans which were comfortably shabby, certainly not trendily distressed. Beady of eye, sharp of tongue. A curmudgeon at worst, a cynic at best. What was he doing even looking at a perky poppet in polka-dotted dress, let alone thinking dangerous thoughts about her.

And yet, Ole Alec did obsess. Every time she looked cutely at him, his heart leapt and then his teeth clenched (yes, he still had all of them). It was bad enough when the eye contact was restricted to out-of-reach hoardings just once a week, or even a little oftener. But for several years now, she'd roused/ruined his happiness in his own home first thing in the morning. She'd started jumping out of *The Times of India*, every morning. Yes, *The Times of India*, which had always been HIS domain, right? He loved her cheeky take on whatever was seizing the public imagination. But man, how he hated the fact that this chit of a girl came up with these punchy one-liners every single day. How did she do it, taking the mickey out

The allocation of coal blocks landed the Congress government, headed by Prime Minister Manmohan Singh, in hot water.

Two good: Angelina Jolie and Brad Pitt make a movie – and news – in Mumbai.

of the good and the great with unfaltering consistency? This utterly delicious kid who looked as if butter wouldn't melt in her pout?

Alec thought he was smart, but this little Amuli was smarter. Harry Belafonte had crooned, 'Woman smarter than de man in every way,' but that fellow was singing of the experienced adult female, not a babe barely out of her diapers. Cute she may be, but how dare she hijack what was *his* stock in trade, beat him at his own game? Not just once in every ad, but twice over. Thumbing her pert nose at him, she managed to slip a second witticism into the sign-off line. She did it seven times a week while he was confined to just his Thursday slot. To rub salted butter into his wounds, Erratica was confined to the bottom of a column on the edit page buried deep into the paper, while this *bachcha* born yesterday had jockeyed herself to pole position at the top of Page 3. What a slight from this not-so-slight creature. No wonder Alec smarted.

Then one day they met. Little Amuli was sitting on a park bench, swinging her podgy legs and savouring a thickly slathered slice of bread. Alec was slouching along, hoping inspiration would jump out of his head or the bushes. Like in some bad Bollywood movie, they both looked up. In her sparky way, the little girl waved at him, and invited him to come and share her sandwich. When he hesitated, she said coquettishly, 'It's utterly butterly delicious.'

Amul's take on artist M.F. Husain's obsession with actress Madhuri Dixit.

'Well,' thought Alec, 'If you can't beat them, join them.' He decided to *maska-lagao* her and see if he could figure out how she'd become such a big cheese. Or at least a block of creamy Amul pun-eer.

As often happens, he came to prey, but stayed to pray at the shrine of her wit. She was young enough to be his granddaughter but, when they got sparring, she came up with – and he had to admit, smarter – Alec-isms. In the face of such spontaneous ripostes, he could no longer hide behind the consolation that those Amul lines were the handiwork of some dyed-in-the-bull ad guy, some Rahul daPunha.

Actually, no one could accuse her of mere puns, rightly dissed as the 'lowest form of wit'. Her humour was like his own USP: not just an empty play on words for its own sake, but always incorporating current happenings. Not a crass simile, but a nuanced metaphor. His and hers was a stylish brand of word play – not rape but

Mike Tyson bit a part of Evander Holyfield's ear off in a bout!

seduction, a contextual fantasy. Old Alec discovered to his surprise that he was now willing to share the bedrock of his glory with such a consummate partner.

He hated it when someone thought they were praising him as a 'pun pundit'. He was quick to replace that description with the one coined by an earlier, discerning editor: 'It's not a mere play on words, it's an intelligent association of ideas.'

Amuli was equally, if not more, brilliant at such layered political punditry. The Coalgate scam became a fun-mine with 'Coalmaal' and 'Amul: India digs it.' The Brangelina couple was toasted with a visual of Angelina canoodling up to Pitt in an auto rickshaw, with the line 'Brad butter' signed off with 'Jolie good fun.' Or M.F. Husain's obsession with Madhuri was immortalized with 'Heroine addiction,' signed off with 'Fida on you.' When Tyson bit off Holyfield's ear in 1997, she had came up with a bandaged boxer and the line 'Ear today, gone tomorrow,' a packet of Amul butter below with 'Packs a punch.' Alec consoled himself by thinking he'd come up with a better play on this adage. After the Congress's electoral wipe-out, he'd commented, 'Heir today, gone tomorrow.' Similarly, the continuation of the dynasty segued into his 'Heir on the G-string.' The jury was still out on who won that other war: Amuli's 'Tel Aviv to stop' or Alec's 'Israel refuses to become Wasrael.'

Then before going their separate ways, Alec and Amuli hugged each other, comrades in arms. They vowed to continue proving that being clever with words is no crime; but a sentence should never have unjustified pun-ishment.

The Palestine-Israel conflicts are a never-ending tragic saga.

INDRAJIT **HAZRA**

Indrajit Hazra is a novelist and Editor, Views, *The Economic Times*, where he writes the fortnightly column, Red Herring.

My polka-dotted girl

Let's be honest. The Girl with a Polka-dotted Dress? That doesn't sound too Stieg Larsson-ish, does it? Now, don't get me wrong. Dragon tattoos aren't my thing either. But red polkas on white? On a frock? Not to mention with a matching ribbon – yes, polka dots again – perched on that fringe? (1980s television pop cultural reference alert... Kitty, don't be silly!)

And yet, and yet... Could I have ever dodged marvelling the sheer chutzpah of the old girl? Here I am still waiting for the right moment and age to wear kajal and step outside, while five-years-older Polka Dots doesn't bat an eyelid – well, she actually bats both of hers to extreme effect – and photobombs her way into pretty much every national and international event worth its weight, in an array of filled circles. To misquote a Ben & Jerry's associate: I set out running but I'll take my time, a friend of the polkas is a friend of mine.

The fact of the matter is, every time I see the ageless, noseless Amul girl in newspapers and on billboards, I don't think of Amul. Or even dairy products. (Although, I do think of her whenever I'm close to any dairy product, a holy cow inside a car or in front of it included.) I think only of the girl.

And whom she's plonked herself with this time. Everything else disappears. No butter. No cows. No Amul. Instead, over the years, I have unravelled the truth about Polka Dots.

Whether it's an irate Mamata Banerjee from whom she's hiding behind a pillar, or a Narendra Modi at 'Modison Square Garden' towards whom she's helpfully pushing a microphone, or the dejected and departing Spanish footballers at the 2014 World Cup whom she's consoling... each and every one looks exactly like the Amul girl!

And once you realize that even Mukesh and Anil Ambani – as well as their mum – look like the Amul girl in disguise, a fact that is driven home by that adjective-defying tag line 'Mere paas maska hai,' it becomes utterly subtlerly obvious that Polka Dots isn't about butter, brand or *bewakoofi*. The world, my friends, is created in the image of the Amul girl.

If you detect the stirrings of a Polka Dots-worshipping cult in my words, a message that the Amul girl is

Mamata Banerjee had a young artist arrested for creating a cartoon poking fun at her, sparking a debate about freedom of expression.

PM Narendra Modi wowed New Yorkers and NRIs alike on his first trip to the US.

Euro Cup and defending champions Spain were unceremoniously dumped from FIFA 2014, their famous style of play not serving them well.

Members of the feuding Ambani family assumed recognizable Amul features, along with a spin on the line 'Mere paas ma hai' *from the cult film* Deewar.

The One prophesied, not necessarily to clean up the world and reboot it, but to pasteurize it by jumping into every other frame of contemporary life, then I am indeed spreading such a message on this giant toast that is the world. The puns adorning her appearance in each billboarded moment – most of them complying with that ancient sacred rule, 'The more horrible the pun the better it is' – are the sacramental ghee thrown in with a swaha-ha-ha celebrating her omnipresence.

The world is round-faced, noseless and, as prophet-visualizer-cartoonist Eustace Fernandes rightly saw in a divine vision in 1966, red-on-white polka-dotted. So if you still think that the Amul girl's 'so cute' and is out there just to subliminally push us towards buying yet another box of butter, you're clearly missing the 'doodh' for the ghee. In dear, beloved Polka Dots, there's something far more valuable, priceless. Amulya.

ANUVAB **PAL**

Anuvab Pal is a stand-up comedian, columnist and playwright.

The nation in a **one-liner**

27 April 1976, around 3 pm, a couple of hours after I entered the world, my father, the non-reclining parent, decided, as one does with infants, to hold me up. The first thing I saw, even before I had time to register who the humans were that would be feeding and clothing me for a reasonable amount of time, was an Amul hoarding. Right across from the hospital. I'm not sure if it was strategically placed there to make patients laugh but it existed, I'm sure, because the powers that be realized that traditional medicines were clearly failing to provide the sort of medical help the Amul girl was providing.

The ad reacted to the sterilization drive going on during the Emergency, which also, unhelpfully, started that year. 'We've always practised compulsory sterilization,' said the ad, but it referred to the butter. It was brilliant. In one joke it did all the things all the newspaper headlines trying to capture the mood of the fuming public couldn't. It made people laugh, and if confronted, they could always say, 'What Emergency? We're talking about the butter.'

A spoof on the mass sterilization diktat of Indira Gandhi's Emergency years, showing the unique Amul ability to take a controversial subject and turn it into a joke.

Naturally, as a two-hour-old, I understood all this. The subtext, the insinuation. I had a wicked smile at the idea of subversive messaging as an alternative to outrage (or – as the world knows it – comedy), and the Amul girl, no different than the Almighty, showed me the way on day one. There was no looking back.

This, of course, is a glorious lie. But for something to be funny, for something to be a good story, there has to be something more than the obvious pedantic facts.

This is something I've learnt from the Amul girl over the years. For a great message, there has to be a world we'd want, a world we aspire to, wrestled out of the world as is, the world we're given.

In India, there's always been the first obvious national reaction to an injustice, a success, a hero, a death, a controversy, an instance of corruption – something on hundreds of millions of minds that week, but Amul always, it seemed to me, asked three simple questions: What is actually going on? What is the real story? What is the funniest way to tell that real story so it is truer than just the truth?

In the wake of the Harbhajan-Sreesanth slapping incident in IPL 1, Amul slapped on this classic.

Applied to my life, the boring truth is that like everyone, I stumbled through life in alternative careers, some clichéd, some adventurous, across continents, uncertain what I was good at, thinking I was great at everything and being mediocre in most. Until finally comedy in contemporary India gave me a home where I felt least useless. The Amul hoarding across from the hospital, however, still stands, and forty years on, still welcomes newborns. So the story, as you will see, is only partly false but true enough to be a story. That's the first lesson the Amul girl taught me about writing comedy. That to understand something, it has to be deeper than looking at the thing itself. That a great story must make people feel something. That there's a difference between perspective and protest.

As a travelling teller of jokes, by default, one travels and there's always a fresh lesson from Amul in how to write a great joke, every week, year after year. Woody Allen, who wrote hundreds of one-liners for a living, said, 'If you make them stop and read the

Yanni came to the Taj Mahal – and Amul marked the event by remixing a popular ad.

The movie Swades *was a pun waiting to happen.*

thing and smile, that's good enough.' Amul's genius was that they went one step ahead. They pushed the cleverness and immediacy of that one line and always, always, connected it to the butter.

So whether it was the cricketer Harbhajan Singh getting slapped ('Pow Bhajji,' with the tagline 'Slap it on') to Shahrukh Khan's Bollywood film *Swades – We The People* ('Swad dish – Eaten by we the people'), to the time Yanni played at the Taj Mahal ('Yanni makkhan'), the Amul ad took Woody Allen's lesson and raised it one level. For us to learn.

And it was always brief. The great dignity awarded to a great joke is that it does not dwell, it does not elaborate, it does not explain because those things ruin the idea. Like spoiling a great dish by overcooking it. These jokes were (and continue to be) served just right, at the right time, to satiate a collective appetite, to fulfil the hunger to react as best as possible, while laughing together. For Shakespeare, brevity may have been the soul of wit but the wit of the Amul girl captures the soul of a nation.

NANA **CHUDASAMA**

Nana Chudasama is a former sheriff of what was then called Bombay, and the author of its most audacious banner.

HISTORY ON A BANNER

What is your earliest memory of an Amul ad?

NC: I have been following the Amul ads since the very beginning. I remember them initially being mostly about the slogan 'Utterly butterly delicious.' A little later, the slogans became topical, on politics, sports or Bollywood. The hoardings bring a smile to one's face. They entertain passersby stuck in traffic. The visual of the Amul girl still looks contemporary, she is so alive! And these ads are all timeless. The good people of Amul may like to know that their brand is my constant companion. I have Amul butter on my toast at breakfast and Amul cheese tops crackers for my teatime snack!

Your banner on Marine Drive and Amul both keep public conscience ticking. What else binds the two of you together?

NC: I began writing the banners about forty years ago with a headline that read: 'Say it fast, say it slow, rationing must go.' It was a way of expressing my views. I call this my legitimate voice of dissent. Sometimes they offended a few, but mostly they were read and enjoyed by all those driving past on Marine Drive. Though the underlying philosophy behind the Amul ad and my banner is the

Amul paid tribute to the legendary cartoonist and his Common Man. R.K. Laxman was one of the country's three courageous social commentators – with Amul and Nana Chudasama.

Amul celebrated the Bandra Sea Link that connects south Mumbai to the suburbs.

In growing incidents of intolerance, regional political parties in Maharashtra indulge in 'tod phod' – in this case against rising toll taxes.

same, Amul has a visual and words to convey the message, whereas my messages are without any visual. I'm a big fluke because politicians actually provide me with enough ready fodder for my phrases; Amul frames clever lines and comes up with charming pictures to match.

Are voices like these finding it hard to survive in an increasingly intolerant India?
NC: The idea behind both our campaigns is the same – to humour people – much like the Air India ads used to (the iconic Maharajah is not remembered much these days, unfortunately). R.K. Laxman and I were great friends, we shared much laughter together. While he sketched the common man's woes, Amul has consistently also highlighted the contributions of the country's best and brightest. Over the years there have been protest voices against increasing censorship. One of my recent banners asked: 'How long will the tolerant tolerate intolerance?' Other questions and observations have got us into trouble with powers such as Raj Thackeray's MNS party, which vandalized our premises here. Though I do think that one has to be fearless and speak out, the best way is through humour. Laughter is indeed the best medicine; the Amul ads know and follow this.

The fifty-year-old Amul girl welcomes advice from the man behind a forty-year-old banner....
NC: She must continue to help people realize their rights, keep fighting for them. I hope the Amul campaign soldiers on with Sylvester daCunha's son and his creative team. Satire has its special place but my banners have been very direct, too, when it is called for. We once had three courageous, humorous commentators who chronicled the times – Laxman, Amul and Nana's banner. Now we are just two.

AGNELLO **DIAS**

Agnello Dias, chief creative officer and founder of the agency Taproot, is a trader of words, a collector of experiences and, by his own admission, the luckiest man in advertising.

The pulse of India is **not** Lentil

'Meet me below the Amul hoarding at Dadar TT.'

Advertising does not normally enjoy a prominent spot at the cultural altar of a nation or its people. Neither pure art, nor pure science, it's generally seen as the fuel that powers consumerism, one of society's apparently modern social evils. And yet, normal everyday conversations like the one above are a powerful indicator of how permeable advertising can be. And how a brand can go on to become a geographical landmark, a cultural signpost, or, for that matter, a Google search of what's on the nation's mind.

Long before computers or the internet, the Amul billboard did, in less than 140 characters, what a global app would do to create billions in shareholder value many decades later. It was shared, viewed, debated, torn apart, adored, commented upon, criticized and loved merely by going up every week. Today we recognize it as social commentary, viral worthiness and content creation.

As an advertising groupie in the 1990s, I can't really remember when I first heard of the iconic Amul outdoor campaign. Back then,

When the social activist broke his hunger fast, the Amul girl offered him food – one of Agnello's favourite topicals.

In 1998, the man who was head of the BCCI was knee deep in controversy. We asked questions which didn't make him comfortable. This is also one of Agnello's top two Amul ads.

it was looked forward to with the same child-like anticipation as the release of the Friday movie or a favourite television serial. You had some idea of what it could be about but you still wanted to see how they would do it.

For aspiring advertising writers, on the other hand, no portfolio was complete without a few speculative Amul pages in it. In fact, it was the section that even the interviewer looked forward to – the Amul lines were their reward for having spent time going through your book.

A touchstone, by definition, is a piece of fine-grained dark schist or jasper formerly used for testing alloys of gold by observing the colour of the mark that they made on it. And that is what the Amul hoardings were for every aspiring writer of my generation – not just a campaign, but syllabus.

Even today, incredibly, so many brands measure the icing on their campaign cake by whether they have featured on an Amul hoarding. Which, in a mercenary brand-eat-brand world, is a staggering achievement by the daCunhas.

It is simply because the Amul billboard can truly lay claim to being a fly on the wall of Indian popular culture for so many decades now. The only other icon that can stake that claim is R.K. Laxman's Common Man. I'm sure Amul would concur, utterly and butterly.

LOVE

PEACE

WONDER

COMPASSION

COURAGE

DISGUST

ANGER

FEAR

LAUGHTER

Often mentioned in the rich heritage of the Indian performing arts are the nine pillars of all human emotions: the Navarasas.

Each of these nine emotions is distinct from the other and yet each is the most basic of feelings experienced by the human race. There is shringara – love; hasya – laughter; karuna – compassion; roudra – anger; veera – courage; bhayaanaka – fear; vibhatsya – disgust; adbhuta – wonder; shaanta – peace/tranquillity. The Amul campaign captures each one of these again and again and again, week after week, through good times and bad.

And when any advertising can do that, it slices through a nation's consciousness like a hot knife through more than just butter.

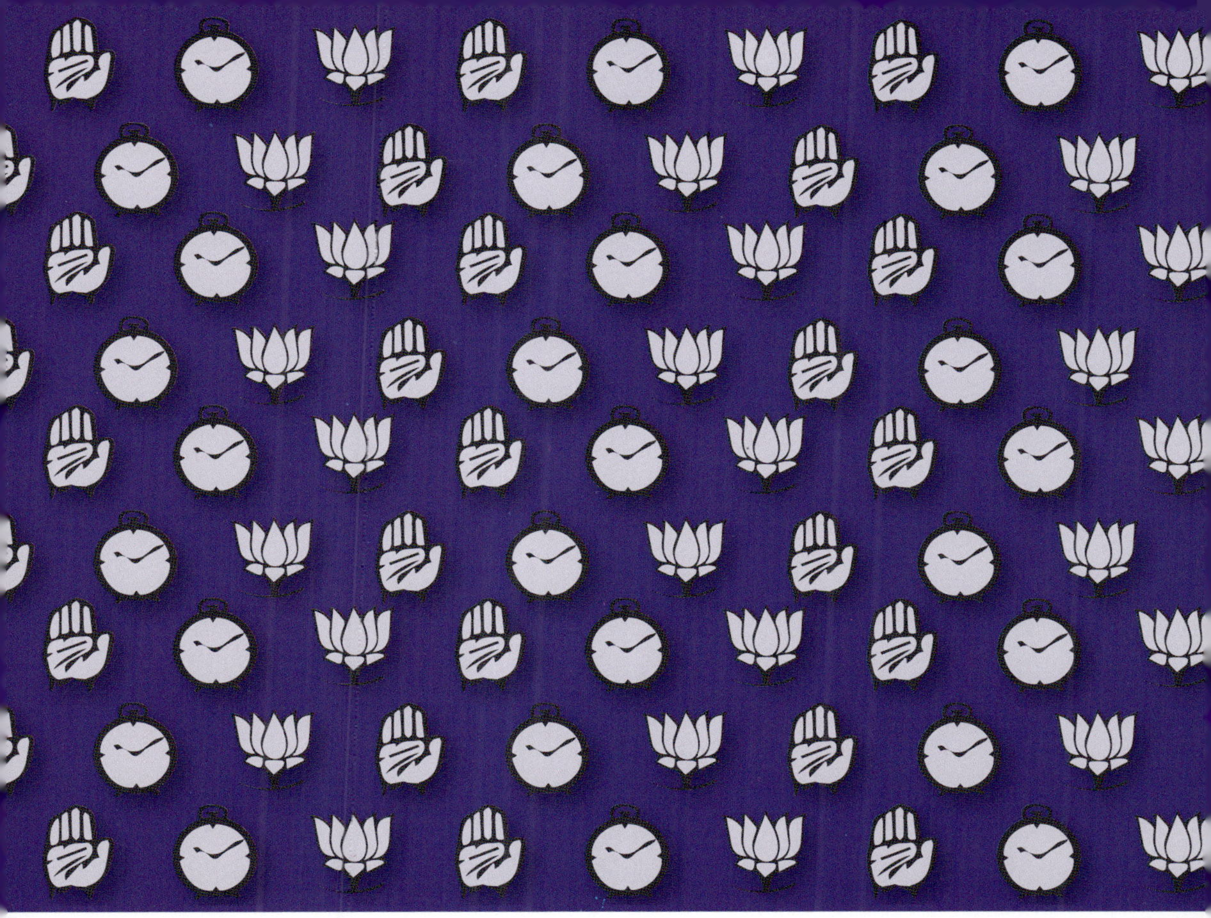

POLITICALLY INCORRECT

NARESH **FERNANDES**

Naresh Fernandes is the editor of *Scroll*, a digital news publication.

Laughter
in the time
of lout-giri

In times of intolerance, can there be laughter? How do you muster the gumption to smirk in the face of the sputtering mob? Can you even begin to bring yourself to be amused by the censor's compulsive desire to deploy the serrated scissors?

India, in 2015, didn't exactly seem to welcome a joke – or even an honest portrait of the state of the nation. Over the year, new laws banned the consumption of beef (a prohibition whose disastrous effects on butter production and cattle rearing will become evident in a few years), undetected caste conflicts spilled into the open and 140-character rumours about religious attacks spread across Twitter like an oil slick. But the nation didn't really want to know.

Shiny India twinkled at No. 140 in the list of 180 countries in the global Press Freedom Index. Across the country, reporters were threatened, jailed and nine were murdered for trying to ensure that the truth prevailed. There wasn't much appetite for wry commentary about national life either. Three years after one luckless cartoonist found himself behind bars for sketches that were

Many celebrated artistes returned their awards in protest against the rising intolerance in the nation.

The All-India Bakchod boys sparked a huge controversy with their 'roast' show.

deemed to be seditious, a bunch of stand-up comics who had provoked a whole stadium-full of people to LOL were served with notices to explain their bawdy jokes to the police – and had to trot off meekly to offer an apology to a Bombay bishop who had taken offence to their cracks.

And yet, how could anyone contain their mirth when reality often seemed to be nothing more than an elaborate comedy sketch? Try to keep a straight face at this: an actor organized a snarling, fist-waving march to demonstrate his intolerance of those who claimed that the country was growing intolerant. An elected representative of the ruling party that is pushing to ban cattle slaughter was found to have made huge profits as the owner of a beef-export unit. At the inauguration of the country's most prestigious science conference, the Union minister for science and technology revealed to the world that the Pythagorean Theorem hadn't been devised by a Greek. It was, of course, the product of ancient Indian wisdom.

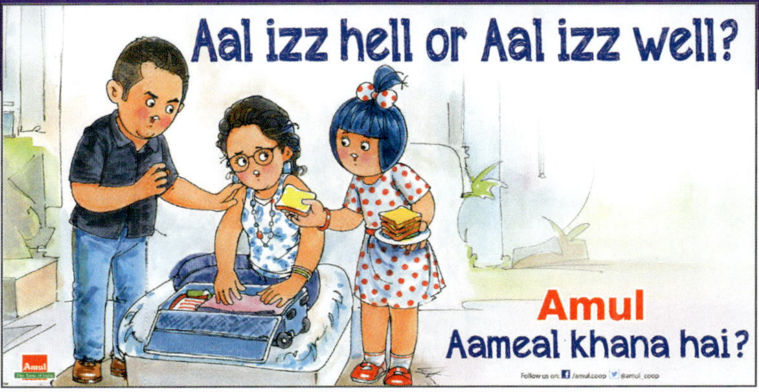

Actor Aamir Khan faced much ire for comments he made about his wife Kiran 'wanting to leave the country' – including losing the brand ambassadorship of the Incredible India campaign.

The Censor Board chief limited the number of kisses in the James Bond film, Spectre, *angering both fans and film folk alike.*

Some political leaders brook no opposition, either from their own party workers or the people.

Comedian Tanmay Bhat's video on Lata Mangeshkar and Sachin Tendulkar was seen to be disrespectful to them both.

Tolerance levels fell to an all-time low in 2015 – what to eat, say, wear and how to behave became a diktat of the powers that be.

But even as full-throttled guffaws were held in suspicion by the moral minority, all was not lost: faux naivety, after all, is impossible to proscribe. How could the self-appointed guardians of the public interest and defenders of the true faith possibly take objection to the wide-eyed inncence of the Amul girl, gazing wondrously at the startling events around her? The cannily deployed pun, the caricature rendered guileless by the soft lines of moppet figures, of these are constructed missiles that fly under the radar, smooth as butter, to puncture political pomposities and bigoted convictions, elaborately constructed lies and dearly held misconceptions.

In times of intolerance, even if no one's in the mood to laugh, a timely incitement to smile doesn't just help dissipate the tension, it can offer the sagging spirits vital sustenance to face the world anew.

Ink-throwing became a symbol of resistance and retaliation.

SIDHARTH **BHATIA**

Sidharth Bhatia, a journalist, author and commentator on politics and popular culture, is Founder Editor of the online news publication, *The Wire*.

A campaign as a country's barometer

A stark indictment of politicians after the 26/11 terror tragedy in Mumbai.

In December 2008, an Amul hoarding showed three heavily armed soldiers guarding a somewhat frightened-looking man wearing a Gandhi cap and a kurta-pajama, clearly indicating that he was a politician. The caption said: 'Will the real terrorists please stand up?'

Three startling things were immediately noticeable about this hoarding, which was put up in different parts of Mumbai and India. First, it was, unlike most other advertisements for Amul, not a cheery quip on a current topic but a somewhat dark and depressing statement; even the black and white rendition was far removed from the sunny and garish colours present in regular ads. Secondly, it was a sharp comment, almost like a political editorial, and anyone in advertising will tell you that, for the sake of the brand, anything remotely contentious should be avoided. Politics is especially a no-no.

Most interestingly, the hoarding was a standout for another reason – though the brand per se was mentioned prominently, it was immediately apparent that the subject had nothing to do with any of its products, and certainly not with butter, which is what most such hoardings are about. It thus broke almost all the rules about advertising.

But then that is Amul. Pushing the envelope for decades and saying – in a pithy and refreshingly different way – what others may think but not articulate, especially not so publicly. Amul's regular ads are an 'Aha' moment; mostly happy and chipper and very occasionally, sad, but always on target. Not for Amul the usual boundaries that form the *lakshman rekha* of advertising and nobody – well, almost nobody – is a sacred cow when it comes to leg pulling or taking a dig at.

The Amul girl has been a canny observer of India through the years; anyone going through the archives over the years will get a good gist of the major milestones of the nation. It's a treasure trove for cultural historians.

At a time when Indians were feeling low and drained after the awful terror attacks on Mumbai's iconic buildings, which ended with the deaths of more than 160 people and injuries to several more, it would have looked silly and insensitive to come out with yet another funny ad. Nor would a cliched expression of mourning do. The city was hurting but also angry. It wanted answers, it wanted leadership and it was not getting any.

The team behind the Amul campaign came up with this hoarding, concise and trenchant and summing up the simmering frustration in the ordinary citizen – why should politicians get protection when citizens lose their lives? Why should three armed policemen guard the neta? Is his life somewhat more special than that of the man, woman and child on the street? Couldn't those policemen be better employed providing us security? Okay, so using the words 'real terrorist' was perhaps a bit strong, but sometimes this kind of hyperbole is needed. And Amul can get away with it.

Such is the credibility that has been built up over years, that rarely has anyone gone after Amul – the agency or the client – for its chutzpah and outspokenness. Even in these humourless times, when people's sensitivities are heightened and irony has taken leave, an Amul ad can say the unsayable, puncturing bloated egos with a rapier-like thrust that gets the message across with humour but no rancour. 'Sanskriti Irani' said one in November 2014, showing the former minister for human resource development, Smriti Irani, teaching Sanskrit to a confounded student, the famous and much-loved Amul girl, while a line

The controversial decision to replace the teaching of German in schools with Sanskrit went well with the name of the Union minister who mooted the move.

underneath said, 'Amul – Swaadishtam snackam.' The trigger was the minister's decision to stop the teaching of German in Kendriya Vidyalayas and replace it with Sanskrit. It was a much criticized move, not the least because it was done in the middle of the school year and was seen as an attempt to impose 'Indian culture' on the hapless students. But the positioning of Irani as a teacher was a sharp idea, given the controversies about her qualifications that were in the air at the time. The text in an Amul ad is obvious, but the sub-text, though subtly hidden, becomes clear too.

Not all of Amul's observations are political or polemical comments, of course. More often than not, a typical Amul quip is a pun – occasionally, a forced one – on some bit of news that is creating a buzz. It has its critics, who say that the creators often stretch the wordplay too far. 'You shawl not do that!' was the line when Russian president Vladimir Putin's gesture of draping a shawl around the wife of the Chinese president became a source of much mirth and a bit of newsy controversy. The Amul girl was there, of course,

Lampooning Russian President Vladimir Putin's much-debated gesture of draping a shawl around the Chinese president's wife.

Riots following the declaration of caste-based job reservations in the early 1990s prompted this line.

wearing a smart suit and beaming at the two. There is no point asking, What Does All This Have to Do With Butter? Amul's hoardings and advertisements have long passed the stage when the product has to be mentioned overtly.

I see the Amul ads as an alternate archive of Indian history, an off-centre look at many major developments over the years, which could complement more formal ways of recalling those times. Poring over their back issues, as it were, I came across two ads from the early 1990s that triggered memories of events troubling and exciting. The first one says, 'No reservation for this quota,' with the tagline 'Amul – The riot taste.' Anyone younger than thirty-five today will wonder what this is all about, but older Indians will recall the turmoil following the announcement that the government would implement the Mandal Commission report recommending reservations for those belonging to the OBC category. Students went on the rampage and some even tried to immolate themselves, such was the anger at this decision that would cut the number of

Amul alluded to the Mandal Commission, whose report recommended the quota reservation rule.

The satellite television revolution with the advent of Star TV was celebrated by Amul with customary chutzpah!

available seats for government jobs. Amul picked up on the anger and riffed on it, showing the girl on the placard enjoying a buttered piece of bread.

The second one was about a development that changed the way Indians consumed entertainment and, then, news. It is almost impossible to recall a time when we did not have the plethora of television channels beaming news, sitcoms, movies, films and raucous panel discussions into our living rooms. But back then only Doordarshan, the government channel, was available. For all its pluses – some landmark shows and sober discussions – it was, after all, controlled by the government, so the news was one-sided; one could call it propaganda. Then came Star TV, bringing with it American sitcoms, music and all the rest of it and suddenly a new world opened up. The conservative Indian was shocked at the boldness of those shows, but saw them anyway. Amul marked the advent of this new revolution with a hoarding that said, 'Out of this world on any dish ... Amul – the Star butter.'

Going back even further is like entering a time machine. 'We've always practised compulsory sterilization,' was one ad in the middle of the Emergency during 1975-77, a dark time when personal freedoms were suspended. One of the government's showpiece programmes was family planning, which involved, among other things, vasectomies – forced, it was claimed later – on men. Freedom of speech was curtailed and the press was censored,

When the city of seven islands was renamed Mumbai.

so the public at large got only the government version of things. The ad showed the Amul girl, dressed as a nurse and carrying a tray with butter on it — government authorities could not possibly object to it. And yet, four decades later, one could well ask if the copywriters were making a cheeky comment on what was really going on behind those tall government claims. This was pushing the envelope at a time when a slip of the tongue could land someone in jail.

There are many such interesting ads which are socio-cultural artefacts of their time, offering a quick tour of contemporary India's history. I find that in recent years the Amul girl has become somewhat obsessed with cricket and Bollywood, but then isn't that true of the nation at large? One can call it exploitative, rather than merely reflective, yet it is important not to forget that the main objective of these ads is to draw attention to Amul. And that they have done successfully, while also bringing a knowing smile to our faces.

ARNAB **GOSWAMI**

Arnab Goswami is the editor-in-chief of the television channels Times Now and ET Now, and hosts the popular nightly show, *The Newshour*.

THE NATION WANTS TO KNOW...

Do you see yourself and the Amul girl as reflections of the mood of vox populi?

AG: With both humour and sharp short messages, the Amul girl has reflected the national mood. On *The Newshour*, I pick up stories that matter to millions of Indians. The Amul ad does the same, too, but far more pithily. I have admired how Amul hoardings capture the nation's attention; they do it far better than I do.

What best describes both your role and Amul's as conscience-keepers of the country?

AG: The Amul ad has not been a please-all ad. On the contrary, it has taken on people in power, taken on politicians when they have crossed the line. I remember the ad after the 26/11 Mumbai terror attacks, which asked 'Will the real terrorists please stand up?' It was a direct questioning of politicians and how they had done precious little to protect the country from terrorists and terrorism. It was a brave ad to put out and I really admire that spirit.

In the 1990s we didn't think twice about lampooning politicians, in this case Laloo Prasad's involvement in the Rs 950-crore Bihar fodder scam.

Amul's question to the men of India after the tragic Nirbhaya rape case.

Amul's digs at politicians always reflect the national mood.

Could the poster boy of Indian television offer advice to the poster girl of Amul on standing tall against dissent today?

AG: How can I advise Amul or the Amul girl? She has done what I do for much longer and with far greater consistency. I admire the candour of the Amul ads. I would like to thank her for inspiring rather than giving any unsolicited advice.

In the build-up to the 2014 Lok Sabha elections, Congress hopeful Rahul Gandhi had a horrific interview with Times Now anchor Arnab Goswami.

M.J. **AKBAR**

M.J. Akbar, a distinguished writer and Member of Parliament, is credited with having launched India's first weekly news magazine, *Sunday*, followed by the daily newspapers *The Telegraph* and *The Asian Age*. He has also been editorial director of *India Today* and *The Sunday Guardian*, and authored internationally acclaimed books like *India: The Siege Within; Kashmir: Behind the Vale;* and *Tinderbox: The Past and Future of Pakistan.*

AMUL AND
THE **AAM PUBLIC**

Anything as witty as an Amul butter advertising campaign must be taken seriously, despite its use of that rhetorical nuisance called a pun. The admen who spin Amul's lines have an accurate pulse count of public opinion.

That's why it works so well.

So when they joined the applause for *Bajrangi Bhaijaan*, a movie that celebrates the triumph of the human spirit over the deepest political divide, it was easy to infer that popular sentiment in both India and Pakistan still prefers reconciliation to conflict, despite acknowledged difficulties. This does not mean it will happen; this merely indicates that hope is not lost.

(Excerpted from 'Bhujangi Bhaijaan: Brotherhood of rivals in Bihar' in The Sunday Guardian, *26 July 2015)*

A stamp of approval on Bajrangi Bhaijaan, *reflecting popular sentiment on both sides of the border.*

VISHAL **DADLANI**

Vishal Dadlani is a rock-and-roller and rallyist of public opinion.

OF ANGER
AND APPEAL

The Amul girl knows what makes people angry but remains appealing as she points out foibles and flaws. What makes you angry?
VD: The thing about being politically conscious and vocal in India is that you end up ranting all the time, because there is just so much to address. The Amul girl, though, is a master at keeping it succinct. She cuts through the BS and gives us reality in a single, funny line. When it comes to political commentary, the Amul girl is like a Zen master – always smiling, always clear.

Which is your favourite political Amul ad taking up cudgels for the common man?
VD: You know what I love most about the Amul girl? That no matter what issues she's addressing, no matter what the big problem of the day might be, there is always the promise of something 'utterly butterly delicious' at the end. That's 'hope', right there.
As for my favourites, the one that stands out right now is where she has her mouth taped shut and the line goes: 'Is the sword mightier than the pen?' Just by speaking up in the face of everything we're facing, she shows that it isn't. She's a courageous little thing.

Amul echoed the fury that most Indians felt at the leniency shown to Ajmal Kasab by the legal system.

Aamir Khan's 2006 film, Rang de Basanti, *defined an entire generation and gave the youth an identity.*

Amul's response to the restrictions on writers at the 2012 Jaipur Literature Festival.

Does the Amul campaign effectively shame those intent on gagging Young India with bans and curbs?

VD: My grouse with young urban India has always been that it is far too self-centred, lazy and accepting of the status quo. However, my childhood friend, the Amul girl, isn't. She's unafraid, she's impartial. She says what she believes, loud and proud. Now that's a true youth icon. May her tribe increase!

BHAIYON AUR BEHENON!

Amul at the Great Indian Political Circus

Arvind Kejriwal won the 2015 Delhi elections by a handsome majority.

Pratibha Patil was elected India's president in 2007.

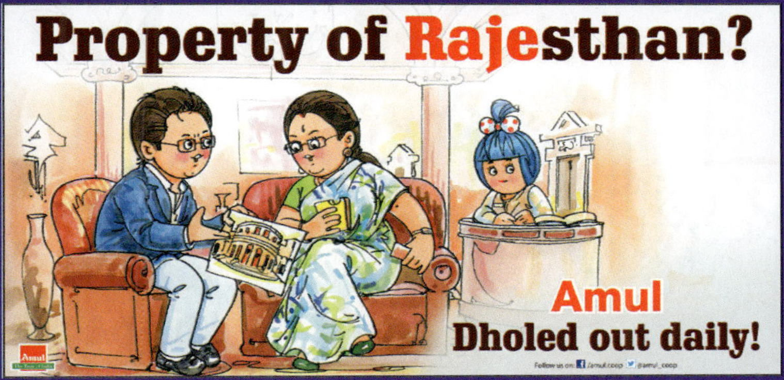

On the controversy surrounding the Rajasthan CM, Lalit Modi and Dholpur Palace in 2015.

The Laloo Prasad Yadav-Nitish Kumar combine swept the 2015 Bihar assembly polls.

Amul humour helps us take a break from Line of Control violations.

AIADMK party workers stuck the Tamil Nadu CM's photo on flood relief material.

Messrs Obama and Modi's friendship aided Indo-US ties greatly in 2015.

Prime Minister Atal Bihari Vajpayee made a historic journey from New Delhi to Lahore in 1999.

This 2013 comment pointed out that problems in the troubled state never seem to cease, but that doesn't scare the Amul girl.

On the successful firing of the Agni II missile.

GLOBAL SPEAK

Amul puts a spin on world affairs

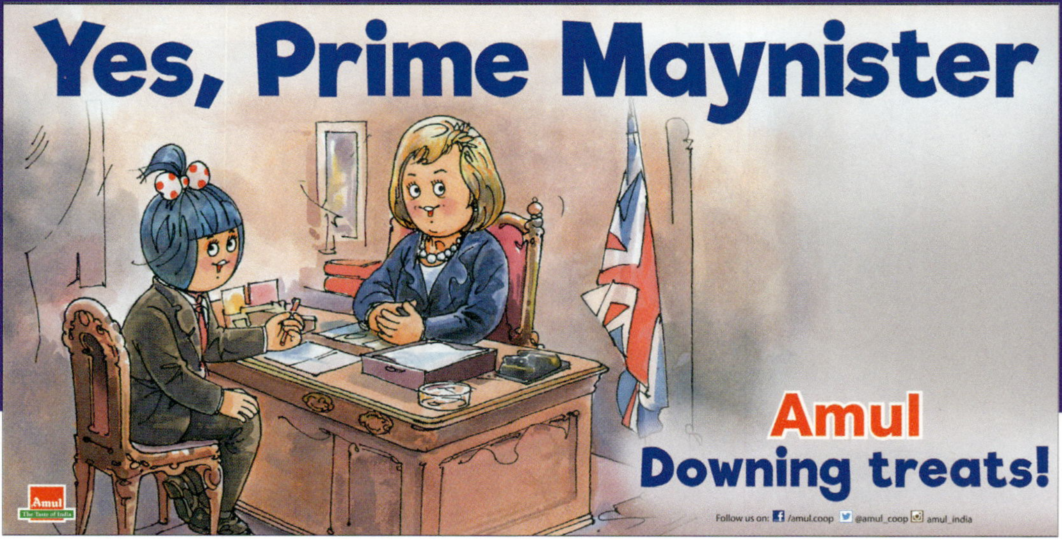

Theresa May became the United Kingdom's second woman prime minister after Margaret Thatcher.

The Republican was the subject of much ridicule, revelry and rancour leading up to the 2016 presidential elections.

The world collectively mourned the victims of the 2015 Paris attacks at the hands of the brutal IS.

The Syrian refugee crisis escalated dangerously in 2016.

Britain's exit from the European Union, popularly called Brexit, became a reality in June 2016.

North Korean leader Kim Jong-un armed himself with deadly nuclear weapons ready for war.

The world – and Amul – criticized the US invasion into Iraq in search of fictional Weapons of Mass Destruction.

The former Secretary of State became the first woman nominee for the post of president.

Obama was the first US president to visit Cuba, in nearly a century.

The Egyptian president was finally ousted from power after a people's rebellion.

VIR **SANGHVI**

Vir Sanghvi, among the best-known Indian journalists of his generation, has a career that straddles print, television, books and now new media. He is a columnist for the *Hindustan Times*, with which he has been associated since 1999 when he was appointed its editor.

Going for gold

If you grew up in India as part of my generation, then you divide the world into BA (Before Amul) and AA (After Amul). In the days before we Gujaratis colonized the butter world with our Kaira District Cooperative (but pronounced Kheda, the Anglicized spelling is all wrong), each town had its own local butters. Usually they were small artisanal operations produced by a nearby dairy which did not have the benefit of Amul's access to modern technology.

In Bombay, we had Polson, frequently sold in tin cans (you needed a can opener to get at the butter) and now remembered chiefly for the name rather than the quality of the butter. (Because the Bombay film industry set the standard for the colloquial, Polson became a synonym for *makkhan* as in *makkhan lagana*.)

At school in Ajmer, we had a local butter that was incompletely churned, so rather than being an even yellow, it had little chunks of cream. Such was our desire to get 'real' butter that we petitioned the Mess to arrange for supplies of Amul. Looking back, I guess we were not foodies in those days.

Serve the same butter now and you can pass it off as an artisanal product that is so fresh that you can actually taste the cream.

Amul succeeded in equal parts because of Dr Kurien and Sylvester daCunha. Kurien's contribution lay in organizing the co-operative that churned international quality butter of a consistent standard. Sylvie's contribution was to make Amul India's first great food brand. His slogan and the fat boy and girl who dominated the hoardings all became an integral part of Indian popular culture. In the process, Amul became synonymous with butter. (Funny business, that a Gujarati butter

should have been promoted by a Malayali and a Goan, no?)

Since then other dairies have begun producing international-quality butter. But on the whole, they have been content to reproduce the taste of Amul. Do a blind tasting of four widely available butters and you will be surprised to discover that they're all broadly similar because market research has told manufacturers that Indians think the true taste of butter is the one that Amul perfected.

Butter can be a complicated business so I'm wary of making recommendations. But remember that there are some things for which no butter other than Amul will ever do. One of these is pao bhaji, another great Gujarati invention... And if you are to make

it right, then you can forget about poncy Normandy butters. Nothing but that most Gujarati of butters – Amul – will do.

Which is not to say that there is no room for poncy butters. You can't bake properly with Amul. You need a slightly sweeter, unsalted butter to cook with. And very good bread demands the best butter you can find.

But for most purposes – smearing on sliced bread, melting over waffles, using as a sauce for garlic crab or merely spreading on a hot naan – you can't beat Amul. It's utterly butterly Indian and it's the butter we grew up on.

(Excerpted from 'Golden Days' by Vir Sanghvi, HT Sunday Magazine*, 21 January 2007)*

BOLLYWOOD
IS JOLLY GOOD

Amitabh Bachchan
is without a doubt
our greatest screen
icon and idol

What makes the **Big B** smile

Over the years, the Big B has been a favourite for writer Manish Jhaveri and myself – whether it's been his wax double in Madame Tussauds, his down-to-earth warmth on Kaun Banega Crorepati, or his colourful array of celluloid characters, the two of us truly enjoy doing Amul hoardings on the superstar – and our wonderful artist Jayant Rane cartoons him with a unique relish.

So when a book was planned on the history of this campaign, we knew it would never be complete without talking to this matinee magician. I was particularly keen to ask the great man if the billboards meant something to him personally. I met him at his tastefully decorated office, in a quiet bylane of Juhu.

– Rahul daCunha

What exactly does the campaign signify to you personally and the film industry in general ?

AB: I think it to be a unique marketing device. Giving the brand a caricature, an emblem, a finite identity and then bringing it across with humour, satire and sarcasm to reflect current affairs, has been most innovative. It is a departure from the straight in-your-face pronouncement of the product. It therefore has a threefold effect as opposed to perhaps one in all the others – the brand, the humour and the topicality. For the film industry and for the films that get mention in the campaign, it's free publicity; a boon for all producers struggling to maximize on awareness without spending. And yes, it does reflect and become a yardstick for success.
I cannot say for the others, but for me when the campaign covers a film of mine, I take it as an endorsement by the public of its success. It goes the same way for failure too.

A tribute to the lost-and-found formula hit Amar Akbar Anthony*, starring Bachchan, Vinod Khanna and Rishi Kapoor.*

Mukul Anand's 1992 epic drama with the star, shot in India, Nepal, Afghanistan and Bhutan, was the first film in Bollywood to use surround sound.

The game show Kaun Banega Crorepati, *aired in 2000, was Bachchan's first appearance on Indian television.*

Amul wished the great actor a happy birthday using two of his film names.

Bachchan, who got the National Award for best actor for Piku *in 2015, with the other awardees.*

Abhishek and Aishwarya's marriage ceremony was conducted between the two Bachchan homes – Prateeksha and Jalsa.

The Big B played an aging lawyer who reinvents himself in Shoojit Sarkar's courtroom drama.

The Incredible India brand ambassadorship moved from Aamir Khan to Bachchan, after the former's remarks on 'leaving India'.

Is it true that you keep a copy of the Amul posters where you are featured?

AB: Yes, indeed, I do!

Where do you feel that the Amul campaign fits into the modern world of Twitter and 'trending'... does it need to adapt to modern technology?

AB: If it ain't broke, don't fix it! Leave the campaign as it is. Change does not always prove successful. The greatest icon of the American hero, John Wayne, never got off his horse in any of his films! The campaign has become, quite inadvertently, the equivalent of 'trending' on social networking sites. It has adjusted itself, without any effort, to the modern world. Great poetry, like great wine, is measured by the number of years it lasts, without change.

JAI ARJUN **SINGH**

Jai Arjun Singh is a writer and critic. His books include *Jaane Bhi Do Yaaro: Seriously Funny Since 1983*; and *The World of Hrishikesh Mukherjee*.

From **Movietone** to multiplex

Browsing through a selection of Amul's Bollywood-centred ads, I passed one, then did a double-take – the sort that Rishi Kapoor pulled off so well in 1980s social dramas – and flipped back for a closer look. There she was, the Amul girl, looking sultrier than I had ever seen her before – and small wonder, since she was made up to resemble the glamorous Urmila Matondkar in *Rangeela*. 'Not Masoom anymore?' asks the tagline, a reference to Urmila's role as a child-actor in the 1983 film of that title. (Back then, *she* could have played the Amul girl, instead of the other way round.)

Masoom, Masoom... Makhan, Makhan. Looking at the ad, I had one of those flashback moments you see in comedy scenes from old movies, where a memory-trigger is followed by an ululating sound and images of bright concentric circles, and you find yourself in the past. I was six when *Masoom* released. The film was very popular in my household – not least because of a conceit that at that age I looked like the cherubic Jugal Hansraj – and around this same time I had a habit of orchestrating little 'picnics' on my grandmother's bed on weekend mornings. The fridge would be

Innocence lost: Ram Gopal Varma's Rangeela *gave us a glimpse of the adult Urmila Matondkar and a taste of bindaas lingo.*

raided, out would come many little plates with bread slices, jam, cheese, occasionally salami...and of course, the butter, always Amul.

I didn't have much brand-awareness back then, but I remember holding the fresh packet, still cool and hard, and rolling the words 'a pat of butter' over my tongue. I was fascinated by that word, 'pat', which I had come across in a children's book. No one would use such a word for butter in my house, it belonged to the quaint, faraway world of Enid Blyton's scones and macaroons and potted pies – but the Amul packet brought the Famous Five's Kirrin Island excursions closer home.

Today, like Urmila, I have lost my innocence: I'm grown-up, there are no fantasy picnics. Some things haven't changed, though. One is Amul, still encountered every day at mealtime. Another is Hindi cinema, which I spend a great deal of my professional life thinking and writing about. And there are the ways in which these two things have intersected over the decades via those delightful ads, nearly as ubiquitous as Bollywood itself.

Romanticizing the past, making it seem simpler and more idyllic than it ever was, is something we all do. So when I look at the older Amul film ads, my first reaction is that they are so direct and minimalist. The one for *Amar Akbar Anthony* (or 'Amul Akbar Anthony'), for instance, has the three brothers in their readily identifiable garb, each biting into bread. 'Roti, Kapada aur Makkhan' has a *neta* in white,

This wordless hoarding was Amul's tribute to the passing away of the great actor, Raj Kapoor.

holding up a buttered slice. Or there is the moving tribute to Raj Kapoor: no text, just the legendary showman dressed up as his emblematic character, the clown from *Mera Naam Joker*, waving out at all of us.

But even with these 'simple' images, you wonder: is the joker wearing an apron? That painted smile on his face, is there a tiny dab of butter hidden in it? A drop of Amul running down the politician's kurta? Such is the history of these ads and our associations with them. You have to look again, and then again, to catch little things you missed.

And in this sense, these ads have something in common with the best of old Hindi cinema: they are unassuming if you give them only a casual glance, but become sharper and cleverer when you look more closely. There is a prevalent view that today's 'multiplex' films have become edgier, more nuanced, having moved away from tropes and archetypes of the past. There is something to this idea,

Shahenshah *was one of Amitabh Bachchan's most memorable screen avatars.*

Haider, *Vishal Bhardwaj's desi* Hamlet *with Shahid Kapoor, gets the Amul touch.*

but it doesn't recognize how many older films, while being products of a particular time and culture, contained unexpected depths.

Working on a book about Hrishikesh Mukherjee recently, I became increasingly appreciative of the layers hidden beneath familiar surfaces; how even seemingly innocuous movies like *Chupke Chupke* or *Guddi* were ahead of the curve in their depiction of class or gender conflicts, how they contained gentle but clear-eyed satire on the workings of our society, even as they operated within safe, domestic, middle-class settings. Gentle satire is something the Amul girl – who would fit right into a Middle Cinema household, a benevolent version of the *enfant terrible* – specializes in, too.

No wonder the ads have never lost their capacity to stimulate and sometimes startle, even though the concept is so direct, and even though the mascot has remained the same chubby doll for decades. The willingness to take on any issue under the sun, the wordplay ('Rich taste se hum tumhare baap lagte hain,' booms

Taare Zameen Par *with Aamir Khan sought to make the Indian viewer empathetic towards autism.*

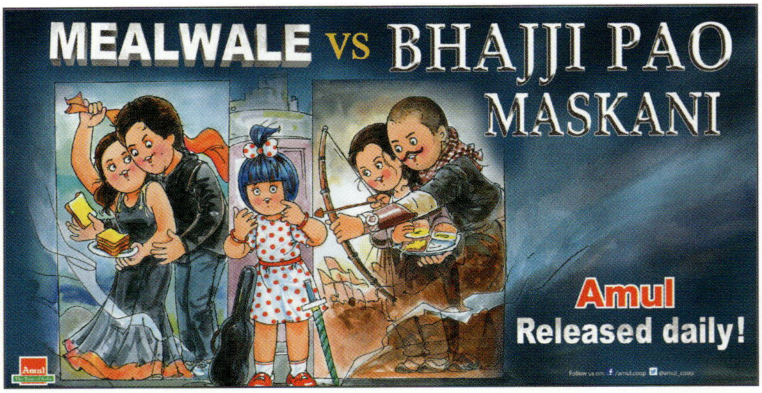

Blockbusters Dilwale *and* Bajirao Mastani *were released on the same day, setting up a mouth-watering clash of the titans.*

Shahenshah 'Amultabh Makkhan'), the little visual touches (the Kashmiri Hamlet in *Haider* holding up not a skull but a plate of a large, misshapen mound of butter – you couldn't call this a 'pat'!), the delicate taglines ('Every bite is special' for *Taare Zameen Par*, a reference to the special-needs child who is the film's protagonist) – it all adds up to lip-smacking effect.

In the past twenty or so years, the ads have been a little more cognizant of how Bollywood has become fashionable and global, and how the conversations about films are no longer just about (or mainly about) the films themselves: they are about the stars, their very public romances and rivalries, their behind-the-scenes doings. The Salman Khan case. The IPL matches. The fact that two big-budget films – the Shahrukh-starrer *Dilwale and* the Bhansali opus *Bajirao Mastani* – came out on the same day. ('Released daily' is Amul's droll description of itself here, a reminder that some blockbusters don't have to be waited for!) They are aware, in our media-saturated age, of the stories behind the stories. They are also aware of how iconic Bollywood references can be used to comment on real-world events in other spheres: the play on the *Deewaar* line 'Mere paas Ma hai' in an ad depicting the split between the Ambani brothers Mukesh and Anil; the use of famous song lyrics in unexpected contexts, such as 'Dosh dosh na raha' in an ad about a housing society scam involving four former chief ministers, or 'You are my Sania' for Sania Mirza.

Amul topicals often use classic Hindi film songs to make a larger point about another issue, in this case, the Adarsh building scam in Mumbai.

And to me, one of the wonders of the Amul ads is that they have managed to retain their charm and subtle wit even while dealing with material that is sometimes best suited to shrill Page 3 tabloids. The moppet has aged very well.

Do I have a favourite? It's nearly impossible to pick, but look at the one for another of my cherished childhood films, *Mr India*. 'Formula that makes food disappear,' it says, a reference to the invisibility theme. That would be a good enough Amul ad, you'd think, but no, the creative team wasn't done, they wanted something more – so they added a little reference to the heroine, an 'Utter Sri Devicious' at the bottom. For me, as an outsider, this is a glimpse into the playfulness and inventiveness that lies behind these ads: how they toy with word arrangements, allow themselves to be cheesy if they think it works, find little moments of inspiration tucked into a sentence, like a dab of butter transforming the texture and taste of a hot aloo parantha.

Anil Kapoor and Sridevi were magical in the comedy drama, Mr India.

KARAN **JOHAR**

Karan Johar has contributed considerably to the transformation of Hindi cinema right from his refreshing directorial debut at the age of twenty-five. He has also found success on the small screen – as a host of *Koffee with Karan*, and as a judge on *Jhalak Dikhla Jaa*.

K Jo

Hai Zindagi

K Jo's first: Aamir Khan's cricket saga, Lagaan, *was a true Bollywood landmark.*

When Rahul daCunha met the quintessential south Bombay boy (alumnus of Greenlawns High School and HR College) in his tastefully appointed suburban office, on a busy afternoon, the great entertainer had just returned from a hectic shooting schedule in London of the film* Ae Dil Hai Mushkil, *with Ranbir Kapoor and Aishwarya Rai.

The young film-maker has always been known to credit his success to his illustrious father, the legendary producer Yash Johar, and his Dharma Productions office typically showcases memorabilia associated with both his father's iconic movies as well as his own fresh laurels.

The popular TV show, Koffee with Karan, *gave viewers a peek into the lives of Bollywood stars.*

Karan Johar's epic saga Kabhi Khushi Kabhi Gham *was advertised as being 'all about loving your parents'... a line Amul adapted with elan.*

Earliest memories

KJ: My earliest memory of an Amul hoarding was thanks to my father. I was maybe five or six years old. Dad would drive me everywhere; he'd drop me to school and then to college. I remember there was a spot on Marine Drive where he would crane his head out of the car window to see something, chuckle, stick his head back in and drive on. As a child I had no idea what he was chuckling at. And in those days all you did was look out of the window and appreciate the landscape and the outside world, unlike today where your face is stuck in a phone. So I ended up doing the same thing later when I was older, as if I was copying my father.

I think the first Amul hoarding on Bollywood I recall was the one on *Lagaan*. I think it said 'Amul Lagaana hai.'

The Amul topicals are never offensive. No one minds them because they aren't personal. It's always a gentle jibe or humorous sarcasm.

This Karan Johar-produced hit impressed the fans as well as film festivals.

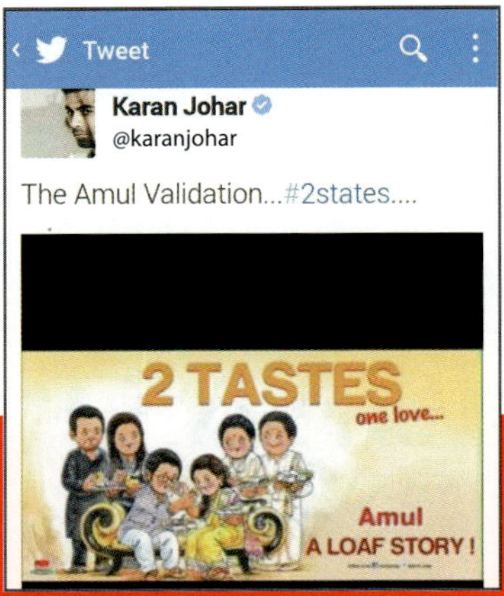

Amul validation

Karan has 8.2 million followers on Twitter. When he tweets something, a staggering number of people read and respond. Whenever we have featured one of his films, or someone else's for that matter, he re-tweets the Amul topical with the words: Amul Validation. I asked him what he meant by that.

KJ: See, we make films because we want to entertain. When you guys cover us on a hoarding, we know we've created noise. There is impact, whether it is good or bad doesn't matter. That is Amul validation.

Amul hoardings stand for three qualities – morality, intelligence and humour. If only our people and public had all three. At the moment we seriously lack humour. We cannot laugh at ourselves.

The Amul girl represents the India that should have been but is not. She truly stands for India. She has aged so well. I wish the country had aged as well, emerged as strong. The Amul girl stands for the triumph of the human spirit.

Cough it out with Karan

I promised K Jo a gift hamper laden with Amul goodies if he could answer a quick round of questions without thinking too much, as spontaneously as he could. He was more than game.

If you were to cast a current Bollywood actress as the Amul girl, who would it be?
KJ: Alia Bhatt!

And who would you choose as the leading man opposite her?
KJ: Obviously Ranbir Kapoor!

Who would you have selected if it had to be an actress from the past, say from the 1990s?
KJ: Definitely Juhi Chawla and opposite her, none other than the Badshah of Bollywood – SRK.

If you had to pick an item number the Amul girl would dance to, which would it be?
KJ: 'Munni badnaam hui.'

What's the first thing you would say to her if you met the Amul girl?
KJ: I would ask her: 'What's your problem? Deal with your issues, just call your therapist!'

Farzana Cooper

NOW SHOWING

Amul goes to the movies

Kangana Ranaut and Hrithik Roshan, excellent actors but ex-lovers, were locked in a lengthy legal spat.

The Bollywood biopic on the braveheart air hostess, Neerja Bhanot, created tears and thrills in equal measure for audiences.

The Vishal Bhardwaj film, Kaminey, *was about a set of twins, one who has a stammer, the other a stutter.*

The rescue mission story of Airlift, *set in 1990s Kuwait, was a runaway success.*

The Bollywood film, Udta Punjab, *about the drug menace in this state, ran into controversy with the censor board.*

Shoojit Sarkar's comedy, Piku, *set in Kolkata, starred Amitabh Bachchan, Deepika Padukone and Irrfan Khan.*

This topical referred to the sinister introduction of the underworld into the financing of Hindi movies.

The 2012 romantic comedy, Vicky Donor, *was about the owner of a sperm bank in search of a healthy donor.*

Priyanka Chopra starred in Mary Kom, *a biographical sports film about the famed Indian boxer.*

HOLLYWOOD IS JOLLY GOOD TOO

Russell Crowe won a well-deserved Academy Award for his role in Ridley Scott's historical drama, Gladiator.

The seventh instalment of the sci-fi series, Star Wars:The Force Awakens, *broke box-office records!*

Ang Lee's epic spectacle, Life of Pi, *wowed audiences all over the world.*

This referred to the seventh instalment in the Paul Walker-Vin Diesel Fast and Furious *franchise.*

Tribute to the great British thespian who strode the screen and the stage with equal ease.

The 2014 Oscar Awards host Ellen DeGeneres took a celebrity selfie, making it the tweet with the largest number of hits ever.

Mission Impossible: Rogue Nation *proved that the Tom Cruise action drama sequels go on from strength to strength.*

Leonardo DiCaprio finally won his long-awaited Best Actor Oscar for The Revenant.

Meryl Streep portrayed the former British prime minister, Margaret Thatcher, in an Oscar-winning performance in the film The Iron Lady.

KIRAN **KHALAP**

Kiran Khalap is co-founder of Chlorophyll, India's premier brand consultancy, a weekend rock climber, and author of two published books of fiction.

Immortality ∞

the dividing
line between
Amul
and **human**
beings

Today's post-internet world of marketing creates a sensation of dizzying speed, microsecond changes, hard-to-keep-track-of rise and collapse of brands. Ok, take a deep breath. Because here comes one astonishing data point.

'Xiaomi Sets Guinness World Record Selling 2.11 Million Phones in 24 Hours'
– NDTV.com, 9 April 2015.

2.11 million in 24 hours!
If that is true, who needs months to build a brand? Who needs years to build a brand?

How old is the world's oldest brand, then?
A thousand years old!
'Since 1040, beer is brewed on the Weihenstephan hill in Freising... Innovative strength and nearly a thousand years of brewing experience create premium beers of the highest quality. Weihenstephan– the taste of tradition!'

It's easy to forget that the true value of a brand becomes evident over time. Essentially, a brand has an unchanging aspect and several changing ones.

If there was no unchanging aspect, you and I won't recognize it. If there are no changing aspects, the brand would be unable to adapt to changes in society, competition, customers.

The Sean Connery James Bond smoked, drank and chased women indiscriminately; the Daniel Craig James Bond does not smoke, drinks beer and weeps for a girlfriend in a society where smoking and sexual promiscuity are not politically correct. But both are thirty-seven years old and British and witty. Take that unchanging aspect out and you might have a Jason Bourne.

Which brings us to Amul. What is the unchanging core of this brand? Fairness to all stakeholders. Here's the MD of Amul, R.S. Sodhi, in *Mint* newspaper on 1 August 2015: 'The co-operative business model is the opposite of MNCs. We buy our raw material at high prices and sell our finished product at reasonable prices. Our model works on scale, whereas corporates buy raw material at low price and sell finished products at high prices, rendering them unable to compete with co-operatives.' Amul: a brand that is fair to the producer and the consumer – a unique brand.

There is something else that has not changed over decades in the Amul mix: the marketing team (led by R.S. Sodhi) and the advertising agency (daCunhas, since 1966). Usually, these are the two biggest enemies of continuity in brands: every new marketing head is eager to display her/his better understanding of a vague discipline called marketing and every new ad agency is eager to display its higher level of a vaguely understood discipline called creativity in problem-solving.

Which is how the delightful Amul girl continues to be the unique face of this unique brand since 1966. Witness this rather explosive mix: a brand that has not changed its core, combined with an advertising property that keeps changing every week!

There have been other famous mascots: Gattu for Asian Paints and the Maharaja for Air India. Gattu may have been junked because changed social circumstances created the awareness that child labour is punishable by law, but even so, he played no role in

The Air India Maharaja worked brilliantly for the airline for so many years, until they changed it.

expressing the brand's philosophy. The Air India Maharaja did – when he was being fashioned by the famous Bobby Kooka and Umesh Rao in 1956. He was cocky, witty, flirty, fearless and did not mind making fun of himself. But over time, he has been reduced to a familiar fixture with no specific role.

There is another subtle difference: because Gattu and the Maharaja have names, the consumer now receives two brand names. The Amul girl has no name, so we remember the brand name Amul and nothing else. But the biggest difference between the other mascots and the Amul girl is in the connection with the consumer's life. However witty the Maharaja was, he was merely remarking on the destination or on Air India's service.

The Amul girl enters our hearts because she enters our lives. She connects Amul and corruption, cricket and movies, our triumphs and failures, our hopes and disappointments. She has transcended her role as a changing expression of the brand, she has grown into a cultural icon. Is she alone responsible for the brand's spectacular growth (Rs 33,000 crores in 2016; Rs 50,000 crores predicted in 2020)? Of course not. The brand drives an unchanging business model firmly anchored in fairness to all stakeholders.

What the Amul girl has done is keep the brand vibrant, accessible to all ages from eighty to twenty. She has shown why brands can be immortal if managed well. But as she once said, 'Zaheer, Ab bas.' So we end this piece and let her continue her spectacular journey.

In the 1982-83 India-Pakistan Test series, the bespectacled batsman, Zaheer Abbas, was unstoppable against our hapless bowlers.

ECONOMY ₹F PHRASE

Amul knows money matters

'Make in India' is a government initiative to encourage multinational and national companies to manufacture their products indigenously.

Service tax rose alarmingly in 2015, causing Amul to plead on behalf of tax payers.

The stock market keeps fluctuating madly, leaving Indian investors in a state of constant flux.

The popular vote was for the RBI Governor Raghuram Rajan to be given a deserved second term in office.

This topical hailed former finance minister P. Chidambaram's farewell budget.

When the Startup India campaign to boost entrepreneurship and encourage the creation of jobs was first announced by Prime Minister Narendra Modi.

The rupee got progressively weaker as compared to the dollar and the pound.

RBI Governor Raghuram Rajan lowered interest rates, giving much needed relief.

HOWZZAT
FOR CRICKET MANIA?

AYAZ **MEMON**

Ayaz Memon is an editor and columnist who writes on several issues, but his first love remains cricket.

On the Ball

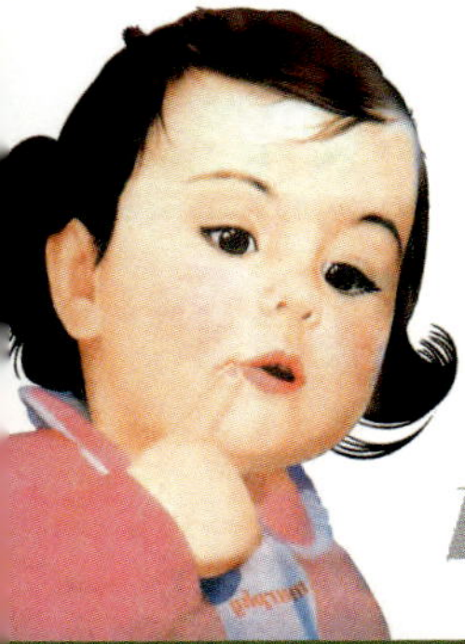

murphy

India has had a few compelling desi icons given to it by advertising: those of my vintage will remember the Air India Maharaja, the Murphy baby, Gattu of Asian Paints, the breathtakingly inviting Liril ladies under a waterfall, to name some. But none, I dare argue, has been as delightfully compelling and abiding a pleasure as the Utterly Butterly Delicious Amul girl.

I can't remember when I first saw an Amul advertisement. It probably goes back half a century when I was not much older than the girl (in her case, luckily, a girl forever) and trying to make sense of the ways of the world – and words. But I can aver that I haven't missed a single ad since.

The hoarding at Peddar Road in midtown Mumbai, at the footsteps of Woodlands building, has been the locus of my association with the Amul world. Driving in from town, it is unmissable unless you wear blinkers. There have been countless occasions in the past, when the city's traffic was less chaotic, that I've pulled up the car at the kerb

across the street near the Vama Store below Kanchenjunga building to soak in the ad, and driven off again with a barely suppressed chuckle.

That was a great pit stop as long as it lasted. Nowadays, you would earn a ticket for traffic violation. It helps when you move ahead a station or two in life and can afford a chauffeur, in which case you only have to ask for the car to be driven slowly while approaching this landmark. With changing times – and technological advances – you don't have to depend on a hoarding to view the Amul ad any longer. It is also available online, which means you can see it in Mombasa, Melbourne, Manchester, wherever. It also now comes out five times a week, showing how the popularity of these ads has grown exponentially.

My fascination for the Amul ad has remained undimmed because it captures the pulse of the nation, as it were. It is uncanny, almost prescient, how it reflects – almost always – what is top of one's mind.

The Amul hoarding has been one of the best chroniclers of our lives: of gain and pain, of effort and endeavour. Nothing exemplifies this better than sport. And no better sport than cricket to give this depth and heft.

I say this as an avowed cricket lover. I firmly believe that no other sport is more evolved or more nuanced. It is a sport which makes technique and temperament as paramount as talent.

This sentiment runs deep in daCunha Associates, I would venture. The love for cricket is not only obvious from the number of ads featuring the sport and its practitioners, but is bolstered by the belief, which I share, that it is also a metaphor for India and Indian life.

Cinema and politics matter, too, of course, but nothing quite measures up to cricket, and this seems to have been imbibed thoroughly by copywriters for Amul through the half century that these ads have appeared.

As in cricket, timing and balance is important in communication, more so if the vehicle is humour. The ads have been naughty, provocative, righteous and indignant, but also humane and without rancour – and, more often than not, on the ball.

Sunil Gavaskar was India's Rock of Gibraltar through the 1970s and 1980s.

M.S. Dhoni inspired India to a remarkable victory in the T20 Championships of 2007.

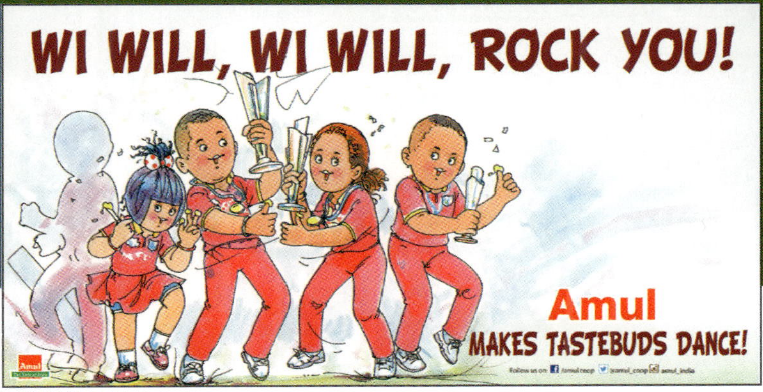

It was Calypso time for the West Indies in the 2016 World T20 championship.

A tribute to Virendra Sehwag after he scored a triple century in the 2004 Test match against Pakistan.

Brevity is of the essence in such communication. An extra word, even a syllable, would give way to an awry reading of line and length, so to speak. A fine understanding of cricket has been meshed with that essential prerequisite of a newsroom: news sense. So, for instance, when Harbhajan Singh and S. Sreesanth got into a fracas in the first edition of the Indian Premier League, what could have captured the event and its impact better than the ad featuring the (in)famous slap, with the punchline 'Pow Bhajji'?

Some other examples which come readily to mind are: 'Toast to the Little Master,' celebrating Sunil Gavaskar getting ahead of Sir Don Bradman in Test centuries, 'India retires hurt!' defining Sachin Tendulkar's swansong in 2013 portraying him as a fuzzy-haired kid, 'Anhoni Ko Dhoni Kar De,' commemorating India's spectacular win in the 2011 World Cup, 'Viru Say Wah,' in tribute to Sehwag scoring a triple century...

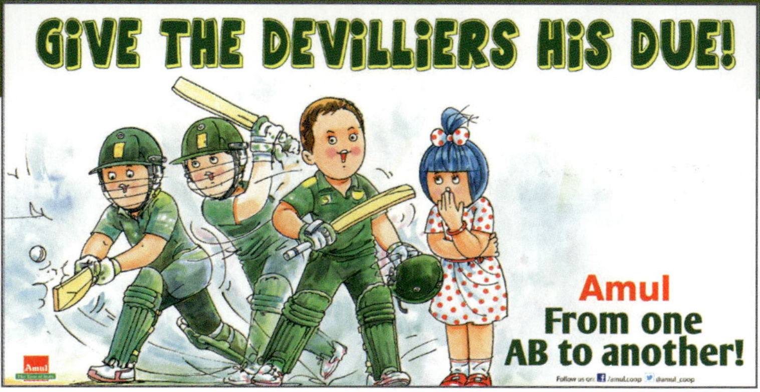

AB, as he is popularly called, reinvents innovativeness in batsmanship.

Actually, to single out only a few is a travesty when these gems have rolled out with the consistency of Tendulkar's centuries over the past half a century. Suffice it to say that they've not just been an advertisement for a product but even enriched our understanding of the game and of life itself.

The Amul girl, in a sense, is both the subject and the interlocutor. She becomes your alter ego: at times curious, sometimes exasperated, at other times exhilarated, at all times engaged, trying to make sense of the world around her. The ads are shy of hyperbole or hyperventilation. Rather, they are, more effectively, a pithy comment on India's state of mind at a particular point in time. The Amul girl has seen us through moments of great tragedy and absolute joy... spreading, if one might borrow imagery from the product she presents to us, cheer in our lives.

Sachin Tendulkar is possibly India's best-known cricketer and certainly the most complete batsman of his time.

SACH **BAT** HAI!

What do you feel when you see yourself on an Amul hoarding?
ST: Amul has been such an integral part of my growing up in Mumbai – especially when it came to street food. The hoardings have also been a part of life in Mumbai. I always enjoyed how the most current topic was chosen and depicted with the trademark Amul puns.

I don't remember the first hoarding which featured me, but it was probably when I had just started getting attention in the media. I recently saw a collection of about seventeen Amul hoardings featuring me, and it was like taking a walk down memory lane as there were so many important milestones or incidents that were covered. I've felt like the creative team has batted for me on certain occasions and simply 'buttered' me up on others.

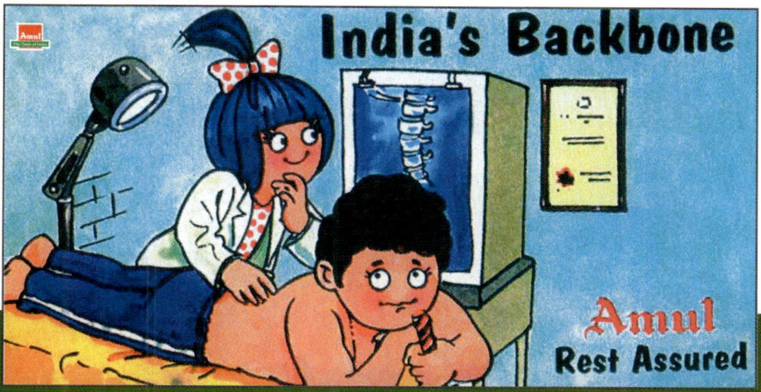

This ad riffed on the superstar's fragile back as well as his being the nation's batting mainstay.

A Ferrari gifted to Tendulkar had teething problems at the Customs.

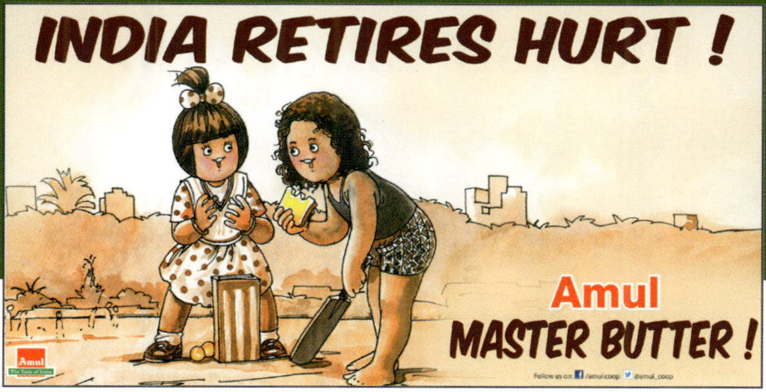

When The Little Master finally called time on a glorious career.

In 1998, Sir Don Bradman compared his own batting style to that of Tendulkar's.

There was much outrage when the Russian tennis star Maria Sharapova claimed she hadn't heard of the Indian icon.

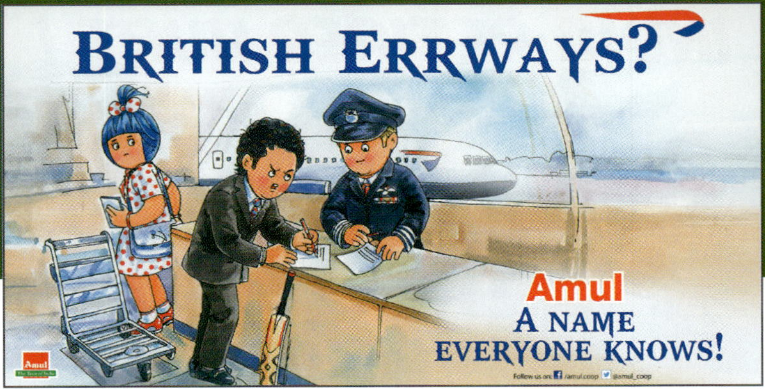

When the airline lost the legend's luggage in 2015, the trollers on Twitter went ballistic.

Hailing the fact that Tendulkar's amazing run scoring was unstoppable throughout his prodigious career.

As a Mumbai boy, what is your earliest memory of Amul ads, and which are your personal favourites?
ST: It's tough to state any favourites, but I used to always catch the hoarding at Babulnath on my way back from the stadiums.

Do you have anything to say to the Amul girl, who is your biggest fan?
ST: I'd just like to say an 'utterly butterly' Thank You to the Amul girl for supporting me over the years, and I look forward to seeing her on the next hoarding! What is the secret behind her staying forever young?

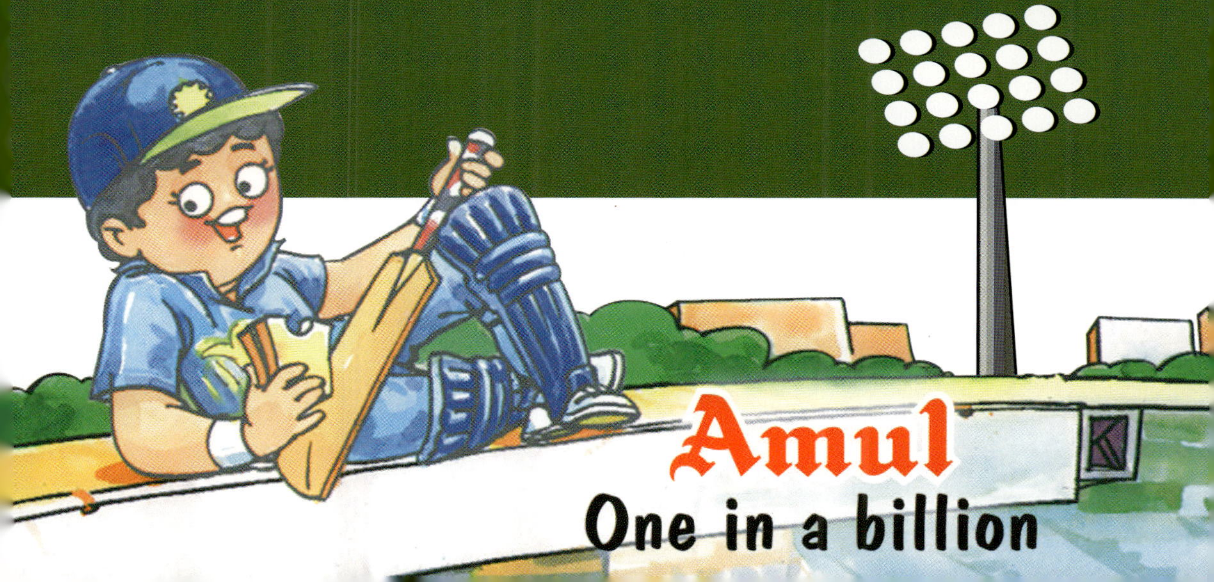

V.V.S. **LAXMAN**

V.V.S. Laxman is one of India's greatest-ever batsmen. A native of Hyderabad and known for his supple wrists, his 281 against Australia at Eden Gardens in 2001 is regarded as one of the greatest innings in Test cricket. He is currently mentor of the Sunrisers Hyderabad in IPL.

FLICK OF THE **WRIST**

Is there a first memory of an Amul hoarding in Hyderabad where you grew up?
VVS: I don't remember when was the first time I saw an Amul hoarding but I always enjoyed having Amul butter as a kid.

What is your take on the Amul ads?
VVS: I feel that Amul ads are very witty, topical, with a subtle brand promotion and also epitomizing that less is more.

Could you describe the feeling when you first saw yourself in an Amul ad?
VVS: It felt great, especially when I saw the ad after my retirement and the headline was apt: 'Laxman draws his own Laxmanrekha.'

How do you feel to be told that the Amul girl wishes one of her favourite cricketers all the best for his future projects?
VVS: I feel extremely happy and pleased to know that I am one of the favourite cricketers of the Amul girl and I thank her for all the good wishes.

When the wristy right-hander retired, it created a hole in the Indian batting line-up that is yet to be filled.

WINNING THE TOSS

Amul's tribute to the Gentleman's Game

The great Indian all-rounder's criticism of Sachin Tendulkar's captaincy was not appreciated!

The West Indies star lit up many a Royal Challengers innings with his sixes.

Virat Kohli often single-handedly led the 'Men In Blue' to victory.

The Hyderabad batsman's 281 against the Aussies at Eden Gardens in 2001 turned a losing position into a winning one.

Arvind Kejriwal and Arun Jaitley engaged in the politics of cricket over the Delhi District and Cricket Association (DDCA).

The popular commentator Harsha Bhogle was sidelined by the BCCI for IPL 2016.

The ex-cricketer cum politician's witty, shayri*-ridden commentary won him much acclaim!*

Sachin Tendulkar propped up India's batting in the 1996 World Cup, while most others failed.

BEYOND THE PAVILION

Amul cheers for all sports

At the 2016 Rio Games, 'Flying Fish' became the most decorated Olympian with a total of 28 medals.

When the Bollywood superstar was appointed Goodwill Ambassador for the Rio Olympics, the sporting community was not pleased!

Viswanathan Anand was checkmated by his Danish opponent in 2013.

The young woman wrestler, Sakshi Malik, won a bronze at the 2016 Rio Olympics, ending India's drought of medals.

Air rifle shooter Abhinav Bindra became the first Indian to win an individual Olympic gold medal, at Beijing in 2012.

The Brazilians were humiliated by the Germans in World Cup soccer 2014.

The Serb continues to dominate men's tennis.

The ageless Indian tennis star continued to win numerous Grand Slam doubles titles.

Jeev Milkha Singh made India proud with his golfing exploits.

The Jamaican Usain Bolt is widely regarded as the greatest sprinter in athletics history.

SANTOSH **DESAI**

Santosh Desai is MD, Future Brands, and one of India's most original social commentators. He writes 'City City, Bang Bang', a column on culture and consumers in *The Times of India*, and has authored the bestselling book *Mother Pious Lady: Making Sense of Everyday India*.

Amul's INDIA

Amul captured perfectly the debacle of India losing a one-day match to Pakistan off the last ball in Sharjah.

'It was Sharjah, boys, not Haar ja!' That is my favourite, if not the most pleasant, memory of an Amul hoarding. The occasion, of course, was India's infamous loss to Pakistan, when Javed Miandad's last-ball six dented not only the personal pride of the individual spectator, but put a lingering question mark in the national psyche about whether we had it in us to face tough situations and come out on top. The Amul hoarding captured our feeling perfectly, using stiletto sarcasm instead of blunt criticism. Of course, this was one of many Amul messages that came out deliciously-timed and appropriately cheeky, and gave us something to chuckle about. Growing up in an entertainment-starved India, the opportunities for amusement were few and needed to be contrived through personal effort. In such a landscape, the Amul billboard was a bracing shock of good cheer, to be looked forward to and commented upon.

For fifty years now, the Amul billboard has watched over India, punctuating its progress with wry observation, heartfelt tribute, sly

A comment on the Maintenance of Internal Security Act imposed during the mid-1970s Emergency.

A crisp observation on the end of the Cold War between America and Russia.

comment and the occasional controversial slip. Its relationship with the country has been unique: unlike the newspaper, which offered a daily account of all important events, the Amul billboard was more selective, choosing the events it highlighted with more care. The considerations were many – the event had to be of sufficient interest, it needed to have some dramatic potential and, of course, there had to be a way of connecting with the brand, however superficial or contrived that link might be. The link with the brand was an important part of the charm of the message, for it gave some boundaries to the message and pushed the agency to greater creativity as a result of this constraint.

The nature of the Amul intervention was often very simple. In a lot of cases, it merely observed events and pointed them out. In a lot of billboards, there is little comment. The act of being a spectator, of merely marking out the moment and presenting it in a manner that caused us to smile, was often the only role it played. Of course, there were occasions when more pointed comment was felt to be in order, but overall, Amul used the platform it had in the national consciousness with restraint, something that has no doubt helped it stay relevant after so many years. By not overplaying its hand and being led away by its ability to frame debates, Amul avoided the corrosiveness that can come naturally to the habitual commentator. Tracing Amul's journey through the decades is in many ways akin to tracing India's journey, albeit through a specific and special vantage point.

With its combination of wry observation, heartfelt tribute, sly comment and the occasional controversial slip, the Amul billboard has watched over India.

1970s to mid-1980s

Between the 1970s and the coming of economic reform in the mid-1980s, the Amul billboard documents the disconnected concerns of a small group. A surfeit of spectacularly trivial occasions are paid tribute to.

1985 to mid-1990s

The Amul billboard covers the beginning of liberalization and the change in the political discourse.

1991–1999

The portrayal of the politician as villain begins to emerge with force at this time, with many references to a series of political scandals and controversies.

2000–2010

The movement towards the popular becomes increasingly pronounced as a very significant proportion of messages draws from Bollywood and television.

Post-2010

Recent years have seen strident politicization and extreme polarization, bringing the subject of intolerance centre stage. The campaign explores this theme in a critical yet non-judgemental way.

1970s to mid-1980s

Between the 1970s and the coming of economic reform in the mid-1980s, the story of India as told through the Amul billboard is an interesting one. Not only because of what it says but also because of what it does not. The Emergency is, of course, referred to, and there are hoardings that refer to the mass sterilization campaign, as well as the dreaded MISA (Maintenance of Internal Security Act). The other subjects and issues covered span a wide variety, including Jimmy Carter's 1977 win ('We are peanuts about you'), Lata Mangeskhar's honorary doctorate (the elegant 'Doctor-ate' was the result), the first test tube baby ('Taste tube baby'), the first Jazz Yatra, the auction of the Nizam's jewellery, Gavaskar's double centuries, the Congress victories in 1981, Margaret Thatcher's election as Britain's first woman prime minister and the Congress (I)'s election campaign blitz in 1983.

The 1970s are usually regarded as the most difficult decade for the country as its founding ideals ran aground and found no competing vision to replace them. From the standpoint of the Amul hoarding, we catch only a fleeting glimpse of this reality. Perhaps the best index of the nature of these years comes in the number of

The Congress (I) emblem of the hand is cleverly used to observe its victories in 1981.

Amul's hat-tip to a young student appointed the first Indian head-boy of the prestigious school of Eton in England.

hoardings that celebrate spectacularly minor events; it is tempting to think that as the national picture got gloomier, the hoardings sought out little islets of cheer and focused on them instead. For instance, in the period in question, we see hoardings about fashionable raincoats in Mumbai, a tribute to Chaplin's *Gold Rush,* a billboard about a vintage car rally, a tribute to an Indian becoming the head-boy at Eton (really) and a strike by resident doctors.

The hoardings of this period also give us a sense of the schism that existed in the country between an India that lived in the metros, spoke and thought in English, and felt more at home with international developments than with what happened within the country. In this period the Amul hoardings are more literate and speak to the small microcosm represented by the educated liberal middle class. The choice of subjects is revealing – there is an enormous appetite for international subjects, and the allusions are redolent with inside references. That is not to say that the concerns of the ordinary Indian found no place in this landscape, but merely that a bulk of the messages were such that they would have made sense to a small group only. For this group, the Amul hoardings were highly evocative of the life they lived and the mental universe they inhabited.

1985 to mid-1990s

The subjects covered in the mid-1980s indicate some interesting shifts. The period between 1985 and 1990 is particularly instructive as the world went through dramatic changes and the Amul billboards stood witness to these. We see a discernible shift in the concerns addressed by Amul, as the focus on politics, international affairs and aspects of economic reform took centre stage. The other big change was the growing importance of popular culture, with many references about cinema and television. The subjects covered included the end of the Cold War, Tiananmen Square, Operation Desert Storm, the Bofors scandal, Ramayana and Mahabharat on TV, the passing of Raj Kapoor, the introduction of the IPKF in Sri Lanka, the Mandal Commission and the rise of V.P. Singh, and of course, the crowning achievement of them all – India's winning the kabbadi gold at the Asian Games.

We often think of liberalization as having been really ushered in, in 1991, but in many ways, the most critical steps that helped bring about a change in the experienced reality of most Indians took place in the period between 1985 and 1991. The roots of the new political consciousness of the emerging classes and the beginning of a redefinition of the political power equation can be traced back to this time, as indeed can the development of the middle class as a consumer segment. This is also the time when the popular voice began to gain legitimacy and started to assume prominence in our consciousness.

This topical applauded India winning the Kabaddi gold consistently at several Asian Games.

1991-1999

Post 1991, the twin forces of political empowerment of a new class as well as the assertive expansion of the world inhabited by the middle class can be seen clearly through the prism of Amul ads. The portrayal of the politician as villain begins to emerge with force at this time, with many references to a series of political scandals and controversies, namely, Jayalalitha going to prison, Kiran Bedi being shifted from Tihar, Laloo Yadav's fodder scam, Narasimha Rao's alleged entanglement with a pickle baron (alluded to by the very clever 'Bhrasht aachar'). The tone too becomes edgier and the hoardings show an increasing comfort with sharper barbs. One that stands out for its cheekiness is 'Party, Patni or Woh?' referring to the leadership tangle in the Congress involving Rao, Sonia and V.P. Singh. It is during this period that popular culture becomes one of the primary modes through which change is experienced. The role of the media in framing our sense of reality becomes increasingly apparent. Hoardings marking the coming of satellite television, the

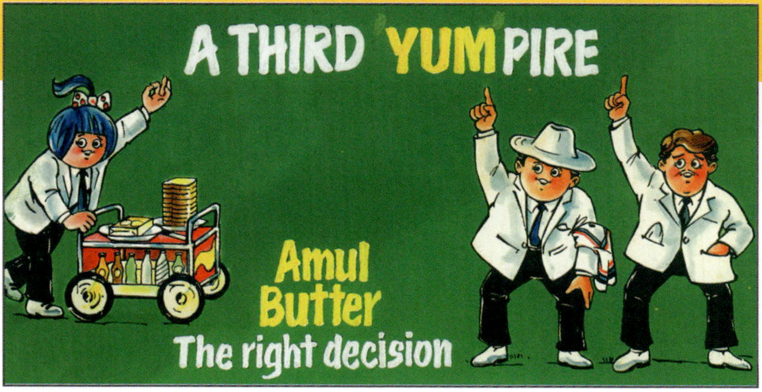

The advent of the neutral umpire reflected the growing clout of the TV watcher.

Amul begins to pay attention to the business sector, as this ad on deregulation of the aviation industry shows.

advent of the third umpire (a development hastened by the growing power of the television watcher), events like Miss Universe and Miss World, the controversy surrounding the advertising for Tuff shoes, all point to this new engagement with media.

References of business begin to creep in, with messages about the Open Sky policy that partially deregulated the aviation sector, the Enron Power controversy, the trouble faced by KFC in its first attempt to enter the country, a nod to Dr Manmohan Singh and his effort towards ushering in economic reform, an acknowledgement of the power of Maruti on the occasion of the launch of Zen, and a heartfelt tribute to J.R.D. Tata on the occasion of his passing, all highlight the growing importance of business and the world of consumption in the lives of the middle-class Indian.

The other notable change we see is in the involvement with the rest of the world, particularly the West. If, earlier, the ads were full of

Following in the footsteps of Sushmita Sen, who was crowned Miss Universe, hazel-eyed Aishwarya Rai won the Miss World title.

Manmohan Singh's liberalization policy encouraged multinationals to come to India and gave Indians the taste of Coke, Pepsi and good times.

allusions to events in the West, in this period, we began to see good news travelling in the other direction as well. The interest in the West continued, with many ads that addressed this need, but events like Miss Universe and Miss World, Arundhati Roy's Booker win, the visit of Charles and Diana to the country, and the (somewhat questionable) achievement of having Yanni perform in front of the Taj, all marked a feeling that India's international profile was on the rise.

2000–2010

After 2000, we see the amplification of existing trends in society as well as the acknowledgement of some new forces. The movement towards the popular becomes increasingly pronounced as a very significant proportion of messages draws from Bollywood and television. Most major new film releases get their own billboard and the overall drift towards celebrities and the tid-bitization of news finds reflection in the tenor of the Amul campaign. We have hoardings referring to a model's wardrobe malfunction in a fashion show as well as the controversy over Katrina Kaif's skirt while on a visit to Ajmer Sharif. The importance of the symbolic over the substantive finds expression in several messages; a sampling includes Amitabh Bachchan's wax figure at Tussaud's, the visit of Brad Pitt and Angelina Jolie to India, and Ekta Kapoor's penchant for beginning her serials with the letter 'k'.

The engagement of the ads with the world of business and consumption continues to grow and we can see how they start becoming very active parts of our lived reality. The UTI scandal, tributes to popular advertising campaigns like Coke's 'Thanda Matlab Coca Cola' and Vodafone's Zoo-Zoos, a comment on the volatile Sensex ('Nonsensex?'), the introduction of the revolutionary Tata Nano as well as the problems it faced in West Bengal, the new VAT proposals, the investment in DreamWorks by Anil Ambani and the war between the Ambani brothers, all featured in the Amul campaign. We also began to see references to the disquiet caused

A response to the Supreme Court of India recognizing transgender people as the third gender.

by rapid liberalization. The impact of flyovers, the proposal to build a mall in front of the Taj Mahal ('Taj Mall?'), the 2G scandal, the Satyam scandal ('Satyam, Sharam, Scandalam!'), all began to find a mention in keeping with the national mood.

The anger against the political class continued to become sharper and the hoardings in this period seldom pulled punches when it came to political scandals. 'Maya ne khaya?' (the court case against Mayawati), 'Beta ban gaya neta' (the tendency of politicians' progeny to carry on the family business), 'Incurable India' (the great CWG bungle), all displayed a streak of undisguised disgust with the ruling class. It is striking that among the several obituary hoardings that were put up during this period, not even one lamented the passing of a political leader. We had tributes to film actors and directors (Ashok Kumar, Mehmood, Johnny Walker, Hrishikesh Mukherjee, Amrish Puri), artists, writers and musicians (Michael Jackson, George Harrison, M.F. Husain, Bombay's own Busybee, Bhimsen Joshi), and people like Dilip Sardesai and Sam Manekshaw, the choice clearly indicating the kind of people that enjoy popular respect and appeal in Amul's India.

Along with greater disenchantment with the political class has come a deeper engagement with the problems of everyday life. The Amul hoarding has started becoming part of the citizen-journalist discourse, as the middle class seeks to develop a voice and make its presence felt in the larger scheme of things. The space occupied by the Amul campaign plays an additional role of

A saucy comment on the stoppage of repurchase of units by UTI in 2001.

Celebrating the appointment of Sundar Pichai as CEO of Google in 2015.

communicating the grievances of its consumers as they go about the business of their everyday lives. Power shortages, bad roads, the impossibility of getting college admissions, even the raising of the legal age for drinking, all become material for the campaign.

The other significant change seen during this period is, of course, the importance of the internet and the many changes this has brought about. Billboards like 'Eeek-mail?' (documenting a destructive virus), 'Dotty about coms' (the dotcom explosion), 'Face-bhook!' (the rise of Facebook), 'i-fun' (the popularity of the i-phone), 'Sabka emotikhana' (the emergence of emoticons as a phenomenon), all recognize the role being played by this new medium in our lives. The increasing impact made by Indians on the global IT stage is also captured in the hoardings. 'Sundar Piyo Chai (Indian Born & Bread)' is a good example of this genre. We also see the first signs of anxieties that have begun to surround the appropriation of the internet by large corporations and the need felt to protect Net Neutrality – 'Tum com ho interfere karne wale

A reference to the high-profile meeting between Indian Prime Minister Narendra Modi and Facebook CEO Mark Zuckerberg.

(Trai this neutralicious snack)' calls attention to this issue. We also notice the first references to issues of alternative sexuality, with a message like 'Out of the closet, out of the fridge' marking the Delhi High Court judgement legalizing homosexuality.

Perhaps the biggest change both in terms of content and tone lay in the growing disease called terrorism. It is striking how the campaign tenor changes when addressing this subject; examples include 'Will the real terrorists please stand up,' showing a politician being guarded by security, a verse from the song 'Seene me jalan, ankhon mein dhuan' and 'Bas ab aur nahin, Kasab aur nahin,' documenting the anger against the long-running trial of Kasab. When it comes to terrorism, the campaign loses its ability to allude to current events, no matter how disturbing, with a lightness of touch. Its tone is in keeping with the larger reaction this subject evokes and is reflective of the times we live in.

Post-2010

The recent political climate in the country, with heightened polarization and the controversies around the subject of intolerance,

The Indian Army conducted a series of surgical strikes on terror launch pads across the Line of Control, in a fitting reply to Pakistan's attack in Uri

has lately been frequently explored. Hoardings like 'Taalerance se taalerance mila;' 'Ink ki shararat (Amul – Splatter this instead);' and 'Yeh syahi nahi galat hai (Amul – Inkredible taste)' that alluded to the ink splattered on Sudheendra Kulkarni; 'Yeh Roasti hum nahi todenge (Amul – AIB-All India Butter)' pointing towards the fracas around the AIB roast; 'Award nahi chahiye, reward toh lo! (Amul – Never Returned),'are all examples of dealing with the subject with an eye that is both critical and non-judgemental, as is Amul's wont. In a climate where it has become difficult to say anything on the subject without attracting strong criticism from either side, Amul has been able to address the issue in its own way without too much trouble.

Overall, the Amul campaign is a very interesting vantage point from which to see the history of our lived experiences, particularly if we come from urban middle-class India. The billboards have, through the choice of their subjects, the breezy manner in which they are brought to our attention, and by the very act of staying current, become a kind of moving timeline marking what we have considered significant at various points of time in our past. The great advantage of the Amul campaign is that it has never tried too hard to make a comment; it is by highlighting a subject with gentle humour and unerring timing that it allows us to think about the event, using our own perspective.

The story of Amul's India is also one of a country coming in touch with itself, even as it transforms beyond recognition. From a somewhat disconnected class living in a world of its own, we see a country create its own narrative, with its own distinctive language, its own set of heroes, its own set of issues, and do battle with its weaknesses. The river that is India flows on, and the brand that is Amul continues to give us a running commentary on what it sees, feels and experiences as it accompanies us on this glorious ride.

A comment on ink-throwing as the contentious new symbol of revolt.

You Tube

VIRAL FEVER

RAHUL **DACUNHA**

Rahul daCunha, managing director and creative head of daCunha Communications, the ad agency that creates the Amul topicals, is a theatre director and the writer of plays like *I'm Not Bajirao; Pune Highway* and *Class of '84*.

Of hoardings
and handsets

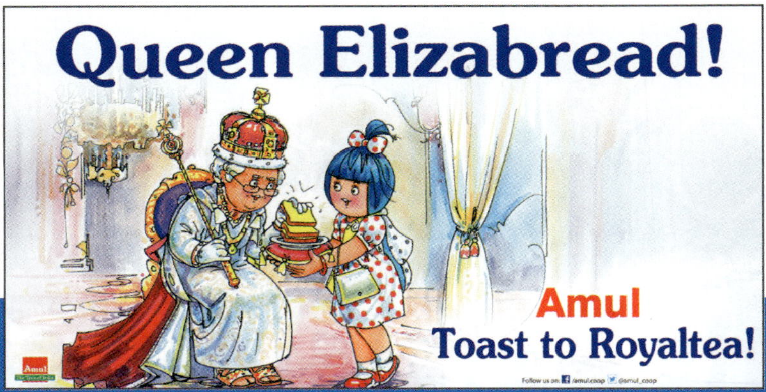

International events such as this, hailing one of the world's oldest living monarchs, tend to be more popular in the virtual world than in the actual.

It's a chicken-and-egg situation: which came first, the bludgeoning tsunami called social media, or the deafening clamour that is the 'new, changing' India? Perhaps they were destined to dovetail in this perfect Bonnie-and-Clyde way. Trollers, tweeters or tantrum-throwing celebs, Twitter has handed them all a 140-character megaphone.

In the pre-digital age, we feasted on events like they were a three-course meal. We soaked the story in, let it simmer for a while, and digested sections of it. We were unhurried, less judgemental, less reactive, single taskers. We had no 'complaint box', so we seethed internally. We chatted face to face, not on Facebook. Now we have a place, a playground to voice our concerns, vent our collective spleens, sometimes we can even lead a 'virtual' revolution, a movement, with a million hits. Cometh the hour, cometh the Twitter handle.

Today we are a nation with a mass ADD (attention deficit disorder). Hot stories are in cold storage by the evening. Everything is an event, everything a potential earthquake.

Arvind Kejriwal questioned the validity of Prime Minister Narendra Modi's Bachelor of Arts qualification.

All this makes it massively interesting for us in the Amul bunker. In the pre-social media era, the Amul creative team waited for an issue to gain national importance. Then we created a topical at a leisurely pace. A wiry gent went up on bamboo scaffolding and painted our artwork on a billboard, safe in the knowledge that he wouldn't have to risk life and limb for another month.

But today it's all changed – the country has become hugely fragmented and localized. We in fact now have several Indias – there's the Northern region inclusive of Delhi and Haryana; the Hindi Belt; Mumbai; the South; the East; and social media, a little country by itself.

Very little is of national importance anymore. Every morning, Manish Jhaveri, Jayant Rane and I are faced with a myriad possible topics, trends and issues to tackle – the Indian Premier League, intolerance, inane name changes of cities, India Shining, Incredible India, new developments in the Indrani Mukerjea case, ink throwing, ISIS

What more can one say about our new favourite animation characters from the Despicable Me *franchise?*

A tribute to the Blues music maestro. A topic like this has huge traction on social media.

brutality, Iftaar parties thrown by the three Khans, Islamabad double-speak, insensitive comments made by illiterate ministers, the 'I' obsession with selfies, Indo-US relations, illegalities, irregularities, take your pick. A smorgasbord of gifts. A bag of goodies all crying for a caustic comment, a gentle prod, a proverb, a pun, a punchline.

We have to decide whether our Amul girl becomes a crusader, a cheerleader or a commentator.

The consensus is that we tackle all these issues. They have traction, they all appeal to an audience. The decision really is how to pace ourselves. The newspapers have given us the topic, but social media has given us the trend, the twist, the timeline. How are people feeling about a particular issue? Are they angry, are they angst-ridden, are they amused? Crucially, when do we strike with the topical – when it is at its hottest, at its most newsworthy, at its trending trendiest. We have to decide when it is too premature, when at its peak, when its most potent and when past its prime.

Superstar Rajnikanth's movie Kabali *broke all box-office records, netting Rs 250 crore on the opening day itself!*

This referred to a viral film on feminism, featuring Deepika Padukone, that met with mixed reactions. The fans called it 'passionate'. The critics labelled it 'pretentious'.

The debate of net neutrality became one that was long argued by the online population. It led to the court overturning the proposed ban affecting freedom of internet choices.

The emoticon, with its playful expressions, became the universal language of visual communication – leading to 'emoji' becoming the 2015 Word of the Year in the Oxford dictionary.

Aishwarya Rai's purple lips on the Cannes red carpet, drew much attention.

The English footballer has advertised many products in his distinguished career.

When the heavy metal band Megadeth came to Mumbai, the headbangers and Harley Davidson bikers went ballistic on Twitter. The general consensus was that we'd created this one specifically for them.

In the seventies, we created one topical a month. In the nineties, it galloped to once a week.

Today, one topical is created every day-and-a-half.

The principle is the same. You have a few seconds to reach your consumer – either he's driving past your hoarding or scrolling down his handset – so you need to catch him quick. Our task is to keep the message snappy and impactful. Never mean or malicious. The mirth of an issue is vital, expressed in a maximum of three or four words.

There is no doubt in my mind that the Amul topical is at its most majestic up on a hoarding. But it is at its most immediate on a handset.

The AgustaWestland helicopter scandal sent seismic shocks over the Indian political landscape.

We said it... they loved it!

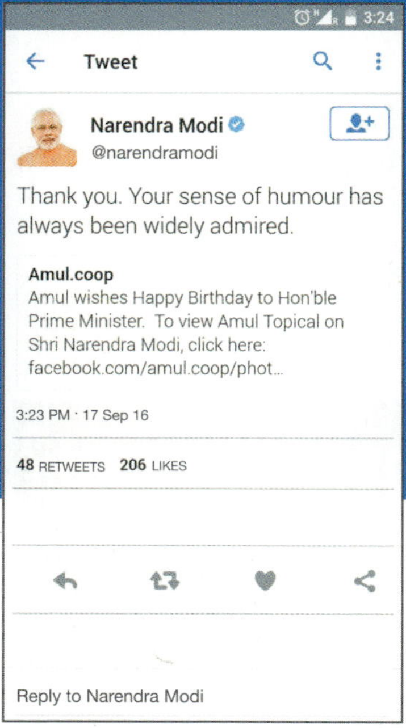

10:36
40456 3G
Tweet
Sania Mirza
@MirzaSania
Amul 😊 love the head band.. ha
Grand Salaam!
Amul
Doubles the joy!
2:48 am · 16 Jul 15
135 RETWEETS 498 FAVOURITES
Reply to Sania Mirza

10:37
40456 3G
Tweet
Shashi Tharoor
@ShashiTharoor
Both my sisters were "Amul babies" in those ad campaigns of the early '60s... now i have joined them too!
Owe for Oxford!
Amul
Bread par
Tharoori hai!
9:47 am · 24 Jul 15
645 RETWEETS 846 FAVOURITES
Reply to Shashi Tharoor

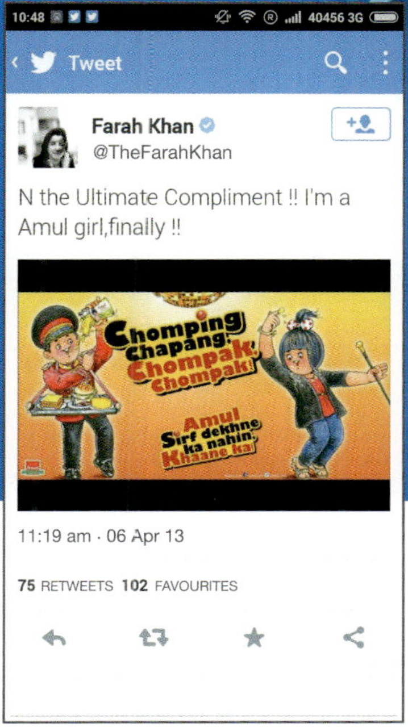
10:48
40456 3G
Tweet
Farah Khan
@TheFarahKhan
N the Ultimate Compliment !! I'm a Amul girl,finally !!
Chomping
Chapang!
Chompak
Chompak!
Amul
Sirf dekhne
ka nahin,
Khaane ka!
11:19 am · 06 Apr 13
75 RETWEETS 102 FAVOURITES

23:31
!DEA-H H+
Tweet
Sankalp Patnaik retweeted
Anupam Kher
@AnupamPkher
Just Landed in London on way to LA. Was delighted to see this Amul Ad on SPECIAL 26. Jai Ho.:)
AMUL SPECIAL
24.7
Asli power iss
1:51 pm · 21 Feb 13
77 RETWEETS 56 FAVOURITES
Reply to Anupam Kher

12:04
IDEA H+
PHOTO
sonamkapoor
1m
DARE HOSTESS!
Amul
BAHUTH, BHANOT ACCHA!
389 likes
sonamkapoor This is awesome! @amul_india
vijayc_7 Good one! Hats off to the artist!
faiz.km 5
desi2wins Check our page for your sketch @sonamkapoor

23:31
IDEA-H H+
Tweet
Harsha Bhogle
@bhogleharsha
Thank you @Amul_Coop. Grew up on the wit in your hoardings. Always bring a smile. To be on one......can't put in words
Harsh on Bhogle!
Amul
All comments welcome!
5:24 pm · 15 Apr 16
86 RETWEETS 367 LIKES

8:46
IDEA H+
priyankachopra
6d
TOAST KHANA
Speak less eat more!
Amul
FROM DON 2 DUSK EAT AMUL
Dil Dhadgne Do!
Amul
Cruise with it!
KOMBATANT!
Amul
Quant some maska?
Amul
Have a PC of bread!
49,054 likes
priyankachopra You know u have done something right when this happens. Thx @amul_india for the constant love

23:45
IDEA-H H+
Tweet
irrfan
@irrfan_k
KYA TALVAR KI DHAAR SE DHAARA BADLEGI?
Amul
PROVES ITSELF DAILY
11:04 am · 14 Oct 15
139 RETWEETS 287 FAVOURITES
mohor majumder
@irrfan_k hi sir
Reply to Irrfan

07:24
Photo
aliaabhatt
13h
No more cut-cut!
Certifiably
(A)mul
70,793 likes
aliaabhatt And again!!!!! #UdtaPunjab #Amul
View all 392 comments
sooraj_9 @aishwarya.asthana @nitienjadhav @trilochanbeheram @vickykumarvky @malwadiadm @soni_sonni @officialyashraj @gulashank @adina_ahmed Follow please this amazing star @marwanyoussefofficial
harshad_mt Congratzzz Dear team

23:32
40456 H+
Tweet
BJP retweeted
Rajnath Singh
@BJPRajnathSingh
This 'Amul' ad reflects the mood of the nation.
AB KI BAR, BHAJAP SWEEKAR !
Amul
PARTY FAVOURITE !
8:55 am · 18 May 14
999 RETWEETS 781 LIKES
Reply to Rajnath Singh

10:12
IDEA 3G
Tweet
Amitabh Bachchan
@SrBachchan
T 2117 - When Amul mulls you .. you have arrived .. !!
A bhi hai, B bhi hai!
Amul
Incredibly Edible!
1:55 am · 19 jan 16
147 RETWEETS 574 LIKES
Reply to Amitabh Bachchan

SHASHI **THAROOR**

A former UN undersecretary-general,
Shashi Tharoor is a Congress MP and author of
several works of fiction and non-fiction.

Amul and the THAROORS

My family's association with the Amul brand is intensely personal. Way back in 1961, Amul's advertising agency, ASP (Advertising & Sales Promotion Ltd), was looking for a baby to front their milk powder in a first-of-its-kind ad campaign. They went through hundreds of pictures of babies – 712, to be exact – until ASP's creative head, Sylvester daCunha, asked my father, his friend at (and secretary of) the Advertising Club of Bombay: 'You have a baby, too, don't you? Mind if you show me a picture?' My father did, and the rest is history: my sister Shobha became the first-ever Amul baby.

History was to repeat itself a year later when Amul and ASP decided they needed a colour picture for their next ad campaign – by which time Shobha, of course, was too old to pose for one. But her sister Smita had been born, and this time, after a more perfunctory search, my younger sister became the first-ever colour Amul baby.

All this may sound trivial today, but it meant a great deal to the family, though the recompense for my sisters' initial modelling stints was negligible. The Amul ads were not just published in newspapers (which themselves had much more reach and impact in those

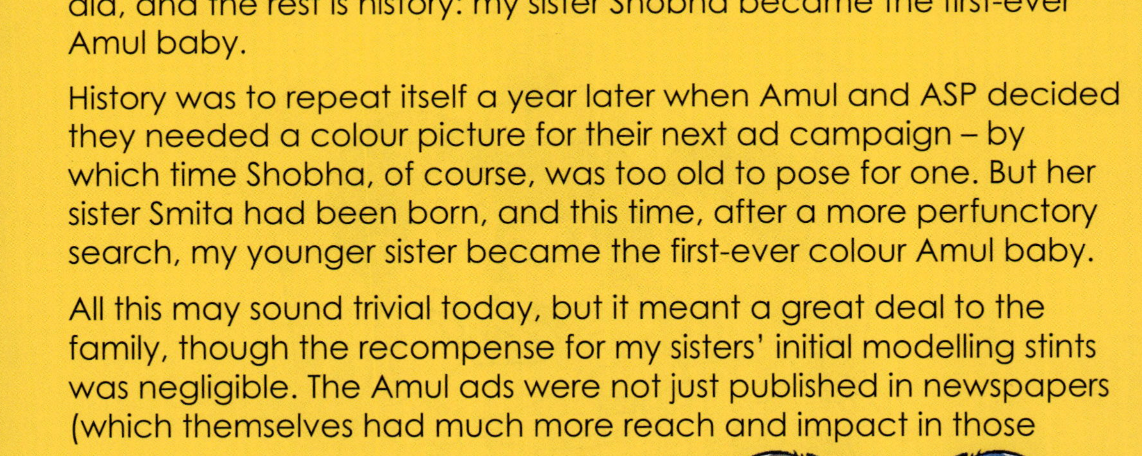

At Oxford University, Tharoor eloquently argued that colonial Britain's prosperity was built on India's resources.

pre-television days), but printed as posters and displayed in groceries and kirana stores across the country where Amul baby powder was stocked. More than thirty years later, Smita was startled to discover a picture of her baby self still displayed on the wall of a rural provision shop in some dusty forgotten corner of the country.

While my sisters (and by association, all of us) basked in their Amul-derived glory, I grew up as a skinny, scrawny, asthmatic boy quite unsuitable to serve as an advertisement for any health-enhancing product, Amul or otherwise. But when, after serving the United Nations around the world, I finally returned to India and entered politics, I found myself in Amul ads as well. Except these were not glowing pictures of my chubby cheeks, but cartoons lampooning me, as Amul so inimitably does to those of our nation's public figures who might be tempted to take themselves too seriously.

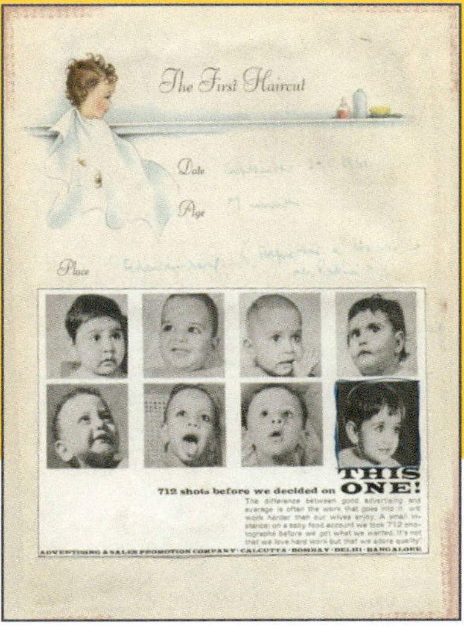

The ASP ad agency recorded Tharoor's sister's selection as the Amul baby in the trade press.

In response to Tharoor's controversial tweet about his wife being 'priceless'.

On the Congress publicly rebuking the Union minister for describing the airline Economy class as 'cattle class', his taunt to the party for its intended austerity drive.

I've now featured in four or five of these, and enjoyed them hugely. They have appeared in hoardings in prominent sites across our major cities, and in newspaper ads, often on the front pages, everywhere. Each captures the essence of the space Amul has carved for itself in our public imagination. The cartoon ads take up a topical subject from the news, draw them brilliantly, and accompany them with a tongue-in-cheek caption, usually involving a pun. And the ad slogan reminds the reader of Amul's 'utterly butterly' indispensability to their enjoyment of life.

The campaigns are inspired, clever, increasingly bilingual, and totally relevant to what Indians are talking about that week. Over the decades, they have chronicled social change in our country, commented on politics and taken the sting out of media controversies. In their quickness, their sharpness, and their topicality, they put Amul in the forefront of the reader's mind. They literally bring the product home to the hearts and minds, not just the stomachs, of Indians.

And in every Tharoor home, therefore, the Amul brand retains pride of place. My late father would have loved to see his son having gentle fun poked at him in a prominent hoarding on his favourite Marine Drive. He would have been happy that I had finally caught up with my sisters.

MOTHER EARTH

FIGHTS BACK

Amul roots for giving nature a chance

Maharashtra's chronic drought situation led to the tragic suicide deaths of affected farmers.

Battle on brave soldier, this topical seemed to say to the man found alive after six days of being trapped in a snowy avalanche in the Himalayas.

This expression of solidarity with the victims of the 2015 earthquake in Nepal tugged at the heart strings.

When the heat wave continued to scorch India in 2014, this was a fervent plea for climate change.

In appreciation of the Indian Army's courageous rescue of pilgrims left devastated by rain flooding in Uttarakhand in June 2013.

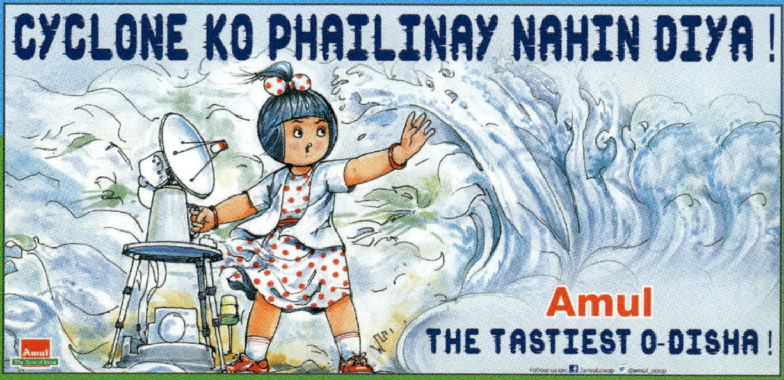

The timely tracking of the 2013 cyclone in the state of Odisha prevented more widespread destruction.

December 2015 saw Prime Minister Narendra Modi and Pakistan's Nawaz Sharif break the ice at a world climate meet.

Chennai in Tamil Nadu fought to stay afloat in the face of relentless and prolonged floods at the end of 2015.

Forest fires raged through Uttarakhand in May 2016.

When polluting fires broke out repeatedly in Deonar in suburban Mumbai in 2016, all of the city was left choking with the residual smog.

R. I. P.

TRIBUTE

TO THE DEPARTED

The Pathankot bravehearts, killed by terrorists at the air force base in 2016, were mourned for their sacrifice and selflessness.

He was a chameleon, the prince of pop, the raja of rock, the genius guitarist. At fifty-seven, Prince was too young to leave us.

The great Muhammad Ali danced like a butterfly and stung like a bee.

David Bowie was an innovator and influence who few musicians in the last five decades could match.

The pioneering architect changed India's architectural landscape. But he was both humanitarian and historian in his approach.

The actress won fans both for her histrionics and hairstyle – she brought the fringe into focus.

Over a hundred innocent children were gunned down by seven terrorists in a Peshawar school in 2014.

The 'Missile Man' was perhaps India's most revered and respected president.

With his pointed ears and paranormal powers, 'Spock' lit up our Sunday mornings as he powered the Starship Enterpise.

Iyengar is still the guru most people think about as they stretch their limbs every morning.

MANISH **JHAVERI**

Manish Jhaveri – the mastermind behind the catchy Amul ad lines – is an award-winning copywriter, scriptwriter and humourist whose canvas includes ads, events, New Age media and TV shows.

SMILESTONES

People often ask me: So how many Amul hoardings have you written?

I honestly don't know the answer to that one. I have been writing Amul hoardings for so long that the numbers are a little hazy. When I started in 1994, Amul used to do about sixty hoardings a year. In 2015, I think I wrote almost 200 hoardings! That's more than three times what we used to do. I think that's a testament to the enduring appeal of these cheeky witticisms.

Looking back, twenty-two years is a long time in just about any profession but in the capricious world of advertising, it is an eternity. Not in this case, though, because time really does fly when you are having fun. So here then are a handful of utterly butterly slices from the last two decades, in no particular order...

One of my earliest efforts, this hoarding set the tone that Amul would follow in the coming years. A crisp-as-toast line with a simple spin on a popular phrase straddling both Hindi and English.

Visually, this was like nothing Amul had done before. The black hoarding was stark and the line, though punny, made a strong statement. This hoarding became a template for scores of dailies, which changed their headline styles and embraced clever turns of phrase a la Amul.

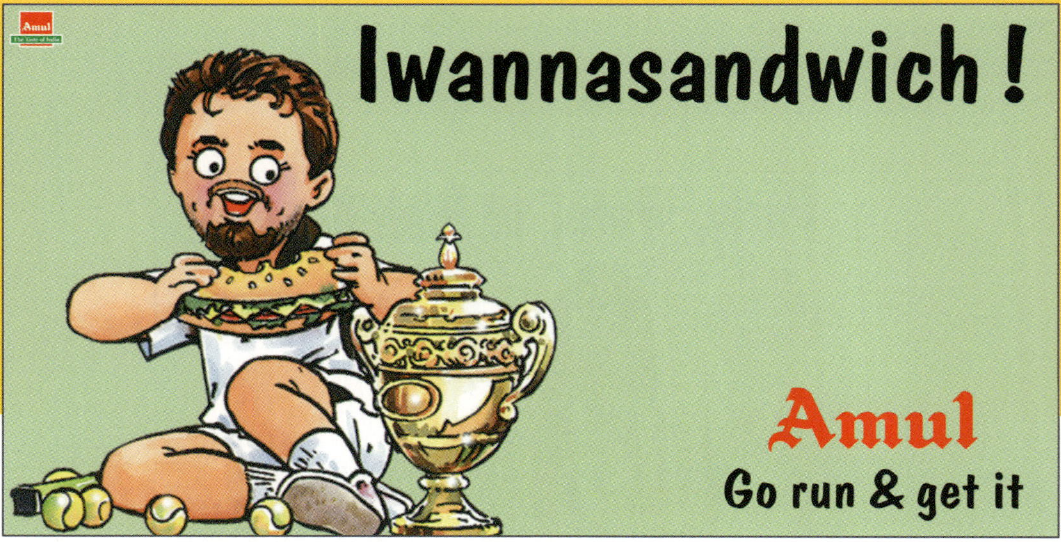

After umpteen attempts, the eternal crowd favourite, Goran Ivanisevic, finally won a Wimbledon title. The next day, I heard a little kid hollering: I want a sandwich, I want a sandwich! And voila, this just clicked! Thank you, little boy.

This riff on Kaifi Azmi's immortal lyric was tailor-made for the musical chairs that invariably follow our elections. From Kaagaz ke Phool to Politics ke Fools ...

To see a Brazilian football team in full flow is to see The Beautiful Game at its most beautiful. This was our tongue-in-cheek tribute to a once-in-a-generation team.

Is this the easiest hoarding I have ever done? Probably. Bhoot and Bhookh really feed off each other. I guess this line was ghostwritten.

Akhtar the Chucktar accused Sachin of being afraid of his bowling. His claim had everybody throwing (now why did I think of that word?) accusations at him. Our hoarding tapped into that emotion. It became one of the most trended hoardings.

This was one of those purely Hindi puns in the 'Roti, Kapda aur Makhan' and 'Amul Akbar Anthony' mould. And yes, Narasimha Rao was India's PM when we did this. I forget what that feeling is called? Freedom of…? Any suggestions?

A very recent hoarding that really had its finger on the pulse of the people. One of the more popular Amul topicals.

Though done around the time when the movie released, this became the most re-tweeted topical, resurrected when Aamir Khan spoke about intolerance in India. *Lekin Aamir… jaana mat, please India mein hi rehna*!

Even Rahul daCunha is probably seeing this 'hoarding' for the first time. My wife Deepa's mother was initially against our relationship. This was my humorous attempt at buttering up the old lady and letting her know that I was really serious about her daughter.

JAYANT **RANE**

Jayant Rane has a diploma from J.J. School of Applied Arts in Mumbai. He has been illustrating the Amul butter girl for thirty years (since 1986) – not to mention everyone else from matinee stars to ministers, from iconic cricketers to international leaders.

Back to the drawing board

TRACING TO
TOPICAL

A glimpse into Jayant Rane's line drawings, from early doodles to the final hoarding at the time of the release of the 2016 film version of *Jungle Book*. Elements and contours changed interestingly as this work-in-progress evolved.

Jungle mein Bhook mitaaye!
Amul
The Bread Necessity!

Amul
Butter
PHOTO
sonamkapoor
DARE HOSTESS!
Amul
ACCHA!
389 likes
sonamkapoor This is awesome! @amul_india
View all 13 comments
A!